MORE TO
YOUR STORY

MORE TO YOUR STORY

Discover the Powerful Experiences You're Already Having

W. CRAIG ZWICK AND JAN J. ZWICK

DESERET
BOOK

Salt Lake City, Utah

Images courtesy and © W. Craig Zwick and Jan J. Zwick.

Library of Congress Cataloging-in-Publication Data

Zwick, W. Craig, 1947– author.

   More to your story : discover the powerful experiences you're already having / W. Craig Zwick and Jan J. Zwick.

      pages cm

   Includes bibliographical references and index.

   ISBN 978-1-60907-228-5 (hardbound : alk. paper)

1. Christian life—Mormon authors. 2. The Church of Jesus Christ of Latter-day Saints—Doctrines. 3. Mormon Church—Doctrines. I. Zwick, Jan J., author. II. Title.

   BX8656.Z89 2012

   248.4'89332—dc23   2012033594

Printed in the United States of America

Malloy Lithographing Incorporated, Ann Arbor, MI

10 9 8 7 6 5 4 3 2 1

To our beloved children and grandchildren,
from whom our joy and learning
have flowed

CONTENTS

CONTENTS

TEACHING TRUE PRINCIPLES THE SAME WAY WE LEARNED THEM

W. Craig Zwick and Jan J. Zwick

Often the greatest truths are taught simply. Jesus taught that way. He did not give lists of instructions or complicated theological discourses but rather simple stories that would shape our understanding of principles.

Principles that have the power to resonate in our hearts for generations need no magnification. And though we may never completely forget correct principles, we do need reminders along the way.

Our lives are filled with short but powerful vignettes that individually may not have immediate or major impact. Often they are forgotten and seldom recorded for future reference. But the fact remains that if in our hearts and minds there is a record kept or a treasure saved, we have opportunities to review, use, and especially "treasure up" (D&C 84:85) those once-forgotten morsels of spiritual energy. Those are the very experiences that can teach us sacred and true principles.

We all have accumulated stories in our lives, and no one's stories are quite like anyone else's. Those stories can contain reservoirs of learning and wisdom. What are we doing with those personal stories of faith? Are we recording them for future reference? Are we sharing them with others? Are we passing them along to our children? Why are the stories meaningful or important? What do they teach us? How have they helped us change?

Our family is as normal as any we have known. We share in the same heights and depths as everyone else. But "our stories" are unique to us and have shaped our lives in subtle yet powerful ways. Each experience shared in this book has provided us with increased faith in God, our Eternal Father, and in His Son, Jesus Christ and in the need to be constantly guided by the Spirit. Each has been a source of a long-term benefit, even though in many of the experiences, there might have been short-term pain, trials, adversity, stretching, and even lack of understanding. These experiences have made up the intriguing tapestry of our lives. Viewed from a distance, this tapestry reveals the broad range of our experiences. Looked at more closely, it reminds us of the singular lesson to be found in individual events. But always an important principle has been demonstrated—something aligned with life's sacred principles and most often taught by the Holy Ghost.

This book is meant to help the reader discover principles of truth in real-life experiences. The chapters that follow are our stories and personal experiences in which we have found meaningful applications in our lives and that have taught us important principles. As our filter for application and implementation, we have used the often-asked question "Therefore, what?"

You may have an interpretation or application of our stories that differs from ours. That is how it should be. In addition, we hope these reflections will inspire you to ponder and perhaps write and reflect upon your own experiences and memories—the significant junctions in your life where lessons were learned and principles of truth were demonstrated. Life is filled with these types of teaching and learning moments, and we believe it is impossible to overestimate the influence our own stories can have on us, our children, and future generations. But if we and those we love are to benefit from these moments, we would be wise to "treasure up . . . the words of life" (D&C 84:85), write them down, and frequently recount them—thus making them part of our family lore and heritage.

Rest assured, we are just ordinary people who are striving to deepen our faith in and strengthen our testimonies of Jesus Christ. We don't profess to teach much that is new, but we do recognize the power in *teaching true principles the same way we learned them.* That is the premise and intent of this book.

Simple stories and experiences that are honestly shared can affect us in countless positive ways. We hear them all the time. We hear them in sacrament meeting and conferences. We hear them when a friend opens his or her heart to us. We hear them at the grocery store, school, and the dinner table. Such stories can help us discover, change, and grow.

> *We . . . write, to persuade our children . . . to believe in Christ.*
>
> 2 Nephi 25:23

Consider a situation, challenge, or unique opportunity in your own life. Was there a point of application for you in the experience? Did the experience make you think? What are your insights, and how might they affect your life and the lives of your family members?

Your stories can teach important messages about your family's values and your way of facing adversity. They can increase your ability to be helpful and empathetic with one another. The principles you learn from these experiences can help you in your spiritual growth and personal development. Your most abundant storehouse of understanding is your own experience. The purpose of all of us in mortality is to learn through our experiences, whatever they may be. Stories infuse our lives with meaning.

The key is to think about our own experiences and then write them down or share them. You may think, "Oh, nothing of importance ever happens to me." The truth is, we don't have to see angels or experience miracles to have something to record or report. Anything that strengthens our testimonies or shapes us or our families is what we are talking about. Nephi recorded, "We . . . write, to persuade our children . . . to believe in Christ" (2 Nephi 25:23).

As you read the stories in this book, ask yourself these three questions:

1. What did I learn?
2. Why was it significant to me?
3. Therefore, what?

You need not be a novelist or a poet to tell your stories and learn from them. As you ponder the events of your life, you will be amazed at how seemingly little things actually teach profound guiding principles that can have meaningful application in your life. Rely on the Spirit to teach you. You will receive spiritual impressions in the process of such pondering. Remember, stories stay with us. The stories of each one of us are important.

Chapter One

THE AWAKENING

W. Craig Zwick and Jan J. Zwick

Road trips are magical moments for our son Scott. A road trip means being alone with Mom and Dad, involves stops along the way for a few snacks, and includes music and lots of conversation. It doesn't matter if we are traveling a great distance or just to the other side of town, for Scott, a road trip is an adventure. He loves having our undivided attention. He stretches his long legs across the backseat and positions himself close to the window as if to absorb as much of the passing view as possible before it slides away. He loves to ask us questions, and they come in an almost rhythmic beat as we travel down the highway: "Why are we going to St. George? What are we going to do when we get there? How long will it take? How many people live in St. George? What kind of work do they do? Are they happy?"

Let's back up a little. To fully appreciate Scott's questions and spiritual gifts, you need to know more about him. You need to know that this six-and-a-half-foot-tall, 295-pound giant once weighed just three pounds. The moment that beautiful baby boy transitioned from the premortal world to ours, we knew he was special. But it wasn't until several months after his birth that we began to understand just how special he is. He is a gift, a noble spirit who fills any room with his presence. Because he has mental and physical disabilities, he can't read or write, tie his shoes, or use a computer; nevertheless, he has taught our family many important principles. Scott has brought us much closer to the Savior and has helped us understand with greater clarity and appreciation the plan of salvation.

Scott has never met a stranger; he just has many friends. When we say friends, we mean every policeman, fireman, paramedic, pet owner, transient, truck driver, or passer-by on the street whom he has ever encountered. Scott has befriended each one without regard to race, age, or socioeconomic status. He is genuinely concerned for each person. His first question is usually, "Where do you live?" or "Do you have a dog?" He never fails to ask, "How are you doing?" And he always ends with, "Have a great day."

Outward appearances don't matter to Scott. For him, everything is reduced to its simplest form. Justice is assumed and trust is a given. Through his practice of unconditional love and unfeigned sensitivity, he teaches us how to extend God's love to others. People respond to his freshness and candor.

Perhaps we can best introduce Scott by sharing a recent experience we had with him. As sunlight began to spill over Mount Timpanogos in central Utah, we rolled down the highway toward Cedar City on one of our road trips. It was a beautiful spring morning, and as always, Scott was delighted to be included in this adventure. Cedar City is located only a few hours from our home, but to Scott, it seemed far away, a place as distant and exotic as a foreign country. After many questions involving Cedar City and the reason for this particular road trip, Scott became quiet. Enfolded in stillness and peace, he was looking out the car window, his gaze riveted on the towering peaks of the Wasatch Mountains. His mood of reverent serenity continued for what seemed like a long time, but it may have been only about fifteen minutes.

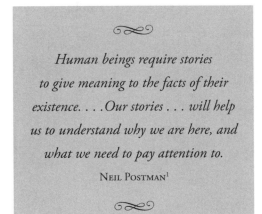

Human beings require stories to give meaning to the facts of their existence. . . . Our stories . . . will help us to understand why we are here, and what we need to pay attention to.

NEIL POSTMAN[1]

When he finally said something, his question pierced our souls and still rings in our ears: "Mom and Dad, do you know Jesus?"

Scott towers over us physically; we always look up to him. But on that morning his profound question, forever etched in our minds, raised not only our eyes but also our hearts to a new level. His simple and direct inquiry—"Mom and Dad, do you know Jesus?"—became a pure incentive for us to increase our knowledge of Jesus Christ and of our Heavenly Father.

So what did we learn from this experience with Scott, and how has it affected our lives?

We appreciated the experience for what it was—a rare and precious spiritual moment. Scott's compelling question expanded our vision and made us think and ponder. It invited the following meditative questions regarding Jesus Christ:

- Have we received His image in our countenances? (see Alma 5:14).
- Have we placed the thoughts and affections of our hearts upon the Lord? (see Alma 37:36).
- Do we always remember Him? (see D&C 20:77).
- Do our children (and grandchildren) know to what source they may look for a remission of their sins? (see 2 Nephi 25:26).
- And do the members of our family see us continually pressing forward "with a steadfastness in Christ"? (2 Nephi 31:20).

Scott's innocent inquiry has also established within our hearts a deep and abiding desire to know the Savior better—not just to know His life and teachings but also to know unquestionably that

Jesus is the Christ, the Son of God, the Redeemer of all mankind. Such faith in Jesus Christ is the fundamental principle of our religion. Every other thing pertaining to our faith is inextricably connected to it.

This experience has blessed our lives in profound ways. We have come to know and understand that nothing is more vital and significant than to know that Jesus Christ is the Son of God. He died for us. Through His glorious resurrection and perfect atonement, we can gain eternal life. That knowledge blesses our lives. It influences every choice we make, and it protects us from the evil influences of Satan. We believe we can come to know the Savior better than we know anyone on earth and that as we do, He will have a greater effect on our lives than anyone else. We know that it is not enough to have a testimony of His existence. We need to *know* Him. "And this is life eternal, that they might know thee the only true God, and Jesus Christ, whom thou hast sent" (John 17:3).

This simple experience with Scott has made a terrific difference in our lives. We hope thinking about it will awaken within you a desire to enhance your own relationship with the Savior. Perhaps it will expand your vision of what you can learn from your children. Or maybe it will cause you, as it did us, to understand that it is not enough to merely remember Jesus Christ; we must also know Him.

Chapter Two

Faith, Not Fear

Jan J. Zwick

It was the Fourth of July, 1989, and we were a long way from home. In reality we were on a different continent, but it felt as though we were on another planet. I was sitting in the mission home in Santiago, Chile, looking out the window and wondering how in the world I was going to survive for three whole years. There I was, a mother with four young children. I had never been to South America. I didn't speak Spanish. I struggled even to say *hola*. My husband had been called to be the mission president, and my responsibilities included overseeing the health of more than two hundred missionaries, half of whom I couldn't understand because they spoke only Spanish. As my husband's companion, I had been set apart as a full-time missionary. Like most newly called missionaries, I felt inadequate to teach others about the gospel. I was totally out of my comfort zone.

Would I have the courage to open my mouth and share my testimony? What did I have to contribute to this experience? Would my children be safe? Why did we have a ten-foot-high fence around the mission home? Could I possibly drive a car when the other drivers made four lanes out of two?

I felt overwhelmed and unprepared. The anguish and fear I was experiencing took up perpetual residence as a boulder in my stomach.

We had just returned from taking the previous mission president and his wife to the airport, and our little family was sitting in the kitchen contemplating this new adventure when the telephone rang. It was one of our missionaries. Because we had been in the country only one day, we had not had the opportunity to meet our missionaries.

The missionary said to my husband: "President Zwick, you don't know me and I don't know you, but I am one of your missionaries. Right now I am standing at a phone booth, and the only thing I have on is my companion's overcoat. We were in a chapel participating in a baptismal interview when seven terrorists with machine guns came into the building. They held a gun to my head and made me take off all my clothes in front of the seminary students who were also meeting there. The terrorists poured floor wax on my clothes and lit them on fire. The building is burning to the ground. What would you like us to do, President?"

That was our very first phone call. I felt like getting on the next plane out of there and was ready to concede that there would be no end to the fear I was feeling. Though the incident happened decades ago, I remember that day as if it were just last week. I remember the concerned looks on the faces of our children. And I remember clearly what I said: "I can't do this!" However, the memory that remains safely stored in my heart decades later was the faith expressed by our then-nine-year-old son, Spencer. With the stature of an adult and the humility of a child, he said, "Mom, don't worry, Heavenly Father will help you do it."

Here was a nine-year-old giving me anew a reminder of Nephi's faith: "I will go and do the things which the Lord hath commanded, for I know that the Lord giveth no commandments unto the children of men, save he shall prepare a way for them that they may accomplish the thing which he commandeth them" (1 Nephi 3:7).

What did I learn from this experience? I learned that I had a choice. I could give way to doubt and fear and let it control me, or I could build and deepen my faith in Jesus Christ. I knew that I couldn't do it without Him. In those three years I learned why it is so essential to know Jesus Christ in a personal and powerful way. I learned that He helps us overcome feelings of desperation and hopelessness and setbacks of an emotional, personal, and even spiritual nature. He will strengthen us when we are simply feeling overwhelmed. He will give us the ability to serve faithfully and to do our best in every assignment. He will help us conquer our fears and gain strength and power to overcome our weaknesses.

This was a challenge, and I realized that facing it would require greater spiritual power. My prayers became more constant and fervent. I searched the scriptures, fasted and prayed, and tried to rely completely on the Lord while seeking for personal revelation. And finally, I tried to submit my will to the Lord's in order to receive His help and guidance.

The Lord reached out to me; time and again He blessed me in fulfillment of this comforting assurance: "Come unto me; for mine arm is lengthened out all the day long, saith the Lord God of Hosts" (2 Nephi 28:32).

As I learned more assuredly that He truly is the "bread of life" (John 6:35) and "the light of the world" (John 8:12), my testimony and sure knowledge of Jesus Christ blessed me in every imaginable way. During our incredible experience in Chile, the promise of the Savior that "if ye will have faith in me ye shall have power to do whatsoever thing is expedient in me" (Moroni 7:33) became my foundation. No, it wasn't always easy. In fact, it was mostly hard and at times very discouraging. It took daily determination and diligence. As a result, I changed. I experienced the fire of testimony that went into my soul in a deeply personal way. I was changed by a profound new knowledge of who the Savior is and what He wants me to become.

I learned not to limit myself by what I thought was my capacity but to allow the Lord to expand my capacity. And He did. This experience helped me understand how true faith in Christ produces hope in Christ—not just worldly wishing but real assurance and expectation.

This experience was unique to me, but I hope you gained some insights or that the principles it illustrates are of benefit to you. Think about an experience you have had when you felt inadequate or alone. Write it down or share it with someone who might benefit from it.

Chapter Three

A TIME OF REFLECTION

W. Craig Zwick

Can you imagine my concern as I waited at the mission home for the arrival of two valiant young missionaries who had just gone through a traumatic ordeal? It was our first day in the mission field, and I had no idea how to communicate with them or locate them. The tremendous weight of my responsibility was made lighter through an overwhelming sense of appreciation for Heavenly Father's watchful care. I waited reverently, with a depth of gratitude for how the missionaries had been miraculously protected after having been caught in such a dangerous predicament.

These two noble elders understood the sacred purpose of their assignment as full-time missionaries. They applied the very principles they had been teaching regarding how faith in Christ leads to action. Their calm and fearless reaction to the threats on their lives was driven by their knowledge of what the Savior of the world would have done in a similar situation. They did not over-react with aggressive behavior but showed love and compassion for those who were prepared to bring physical harm to them and others. Their combined faith in Jesus Christ became a powerful and real protection to them in time of imminent danger.

Their power and authority to act in the name of Jesus Christ, being led by the Spirit to do and say what the Lord would have them say at just the right moment (see D&C 84:85), truly saved their lives.

This explosive introduction to life as a mission president taught my family and me powerful principles. The Javiera Carrera Branch was a fledgling little branch of the Church. Fewer than thirty-five members faithfully attended the branch each Sunday. It was part of the La Florida Stake in Santiago but was often ne-glected; it struggled because of low attendance and lack of lead-ership.

It was the branch council of the Javiera Carrera Branch that provided my first exposure to the remarkable faith, grit, and char-acter of our Chilean brothers and sisters. Our two youngest sons, Darin and Spencer, accompanied me as I traveled late one eve-ning to the scene of this horrific fire less than twenty-four hours after it had happened. With only an approximate address and no GPS assistance to guide us, we arrived at the charred scene an hour later than planned. The odor of burned rubble was no-ticeable as we walked the final two blocks to the site, which one day earlier had been a beautiful chapel. The only remnants of the building were a collection of chairs that had been removed from the cultural hall, three paintings with charred frames that came out of the Relief Society and Primary rooms, and a piano, all of which had been carried from the fiery inferno at great risk of life.

As we approached the apparent foundation and blackened remnants of the building, a dim light was coming from an old mechanical storage area. We could see three heavily damaged and fragile block walls still standing but without any roof overhead. Steel debris was dangling from what had been the ceiling. Inside this partially enclosed space, we found the branch president and his assembled—and complete—branch council. At that moment my boys and I sensed just how significant this physical and emotional loss really was. We will never forget the rank odor and stillness of that night.

These eight branch leaders, representing the branch presidency and the priesthood and auxiliary leadership, had met that evening in the charred remains of their meetinghouse to discuss their plight and develop an immediate plan of faith and action. Those plans included where they would meet on Sunday for church and how they would sort out recovery details while preserving their normal meeting schedule. Sunday would be fast and testimony meeting, and the council decided that with about seventy-five chairs that had been saved from the fire, they would be able to hold a sacrament meeting outside.

The most important principle, however, for my boys and me to learn came when these eight members of the branch council knelt in prayer and invited us to join them. We all knelt together on the soot-covered concrete floor. Then, in a language completely foreign to my sons, President Patricio G Latorre Orellana offered a humble prayer of thanks and supplication to the Lord. It was one of those rare images that cut and paste themselves permanently into the journal of your heart.

In that prayer offered by candlelight in the open air of an uncovered mechanical equipment room, President Latorre asked Heavenly Father to bring peace to each council member's heart and to bless them to be able to forgive the terrorists who had so brazenly entered and destroyed their beautiful chapel. The prayer contained nothing about capturing the terrorists or punishing them; rather, it was all about these pure Chilean hearts having enough spiritual maturity to forgive those who had despitefully used them. As this humble prayer was being offered, we each experienced a peaceful feeling as though God the Father and Jesus Christ were right there teaching us and allowing us to share in this powerful point of beginning to our mission experience and life in the Chile Santiago South Mission.

As all joined in "amen" at the end of the prayer, I recognized that there was a much more important reason for me to be there that night than to just participate as a supportive new mission president. I was there to learn principles of faith and forgiveness that would help me through the next three years of our service among the faithful Saints and missionaries of the Chile Santiago South Mission.

The principle of forgiveness was taught to me more effectively that chilly July winter night in Javiera Carrera, Chile, than at any other time before or since.

We knew the Church would be able to provide the faithful Saints with physical, emotional, and temporal help, but we immediately became aware of just how much these pure Chilean people would be able to teach us about what really matters and about how a loving Heavenly Father listens to the humble and sincere prayer of those who love Him and who love and honor the name and mission of Jesus Christ. They were in serious need, and they knew they could count on Heavenly Father's help.

We shed tears of gratitude with them that night. They perhaps thought we were shedding tears of sorrow for the loss of the building, but our tears were tears of gratitude for the lessons we were being taught under candlelight about faith in Jesus Christ and in His matchless love for all of God's children.

Darin, then twelve years of age, and nine-year-old Spencer, both grew that night in their own faith because of what they saw and felt. We processed the events of the evening and started to see that the hand of the Lord would teach us all by our individual trials and adversity. "The Lord did visit them with his Spirit, and said unto them: Be comforted. And they were comforted" (Alma 17:10).

We returned as a family to the Javiera Carrera chapel site three days later for the branch's scheduled sacrament meeting. It was once again a cold July day, rainy and overcast, but the warmth of the experience will never be forgotten. The meeting was held on the grass, dirt, and pavement adjacent to the burned-out building. The steel chairs were placed on the grass, and the piano was well located so it could be heard. There was no pulpit or sound system, but a table had been borrowed in order to administer the sacrament. My wife and I, along with our son Scott, occupied three of the chairs, and our other three children sat next to us on the grass. We arrived about twenty minutes early, but there were already more than one hundred people assembled. Remember, this was a branch with fewer than thirty-five active members typically attending.

By the time the meeting was to start, more than two hundred people were there for the fast and testimony meeting. We were overwhelmed with the depth of reverence and the happy countenances of those who attended. They came in full support of the faithful core of people who normally attended Sunday services and who had experienced this direct loss. Among those who came were neighbors, friends of active members, and many not of our faith who had genuine empathy for all that had been lost.

A sacred, peaceful feeling permeated the meeting. During the blessing and passing of the sacrament, we felt a sublime reverence that we will never forget. It was a feeling of "be still, and know" (Psalm 46:10) and of "I am with you alway" (Matthew 28:20), which made the experience powerful for our children and us.

As people bore testimonies, we experienced a feeling of gratitude for the Savior's matchless love. Everyone in attendance experienced a level of understanding and trust that established a powerful and undeniable witness that Jesus Christ is our living Savior and that God the Father loves each of us. Several spoke about patiently enduring and reaching out to provide spiritual support to others during good times and during times of need.

The testimonies were simple yet profound. They came from those of our faith and from those who had never even been inside the destroyed meetinghouse. Words of appreciation, encouragement, and forgiveness came from less-active members as well as from the most faithful members of the branch.

Three weeks after our first Sunday experience in Chile, spent on metal chairs outside at Javiera Carrera, we received a phone call from Elder Richard G. Scott of the Quorum of the Twelve Apostles. Elder Scott surprised us by saying that he was planning to be in Chile a few weeks later, in mid-August.

Elder Scott did come, and we shared with him what we had learned from these faithful people of the Javiera Carrera Branch. He wanted to attend a sacrament meeting with those good people. The branch was meeting temporarily in a chapel located two bus rides away for most members. We drove with Elder Scott to the building and entered to find more than one hundred faithful Chileans prepared to worship and partake of the sacrament. They were not aware beforehand that an Apostle of the Lord Jesus Christ would be attending their meeting.

Elder Scott was so warm and gracious with these wonderful people. He spoke to them about faith in Jesus Christ and about the permanency of their testimonies. He commended them for their examples of love for the Savior and for each other. He pronounced an apostolic blessing on the people, promising them that they would continue to expand in faith and in numbers. He promised them in the name of Jesus Christ that they would grow to be multiple strong units in the Church and would become an "ensign to [their] nation."[1]

The ensuing weeks and months did bring growth to the Javiera Carrera Branch. By the first month of 1990, only six months after the fire, the branch had grown by convert baptisms and member reactivations into a solid ward. In fulfillment of Elder Scott's blessing, the ward grew from one to two. Eventually, the two wards expanded to three wards and a branch. By May 1992, less than three years after that memorable night in July 1989, papers were submitted for the creation of the Javiera Carrera Chile Stake. Miraculously, an entire stake was created from approximately the same geographic area of the original Javiera Carrera Branch.

We look back upon this miracle as a gift from on high to the faithful members who never sought anything for themselves. These great latter-day pioneers of Santiago, Chile, were exemplary in overcoming adversity and in placing their trust in the Lord to not only establish the Church in their little branch but also to establish the gospel in their hearts and homes.

Embedded in this experience of our first few days in Santiago, Chile, are many lessons, including the following three.

First, it is essential to know Jesus Christ and to trust in His redeeming love. We learned that the two extraordinary missionaries held at gunpoint not only had faith in Jesus Christ but also trust in the voice of the Spirit, which they responded to as it guided them to safety. A certain level of humility and embarrassment were forced upon them in this unexpected situation, especially the demand to disrobe in front of the seminary students. But they knew their Savior and knew He would not abandon them in their moment of need. In fact, their faith in Jesus Christ, combined with their knowledge of His attributes, helped this miracle to take place, according to the Lord's will. Their faith in Him allowed them to overcome doubt and fear.

Second, the principle of forgiveness is vital if we are to grow. This principle was taught in such a meaningful way by the humble Javiera Carrera Branch council and branch members. They faced a trial and could have reacted with bitterness and anger. They could have dwelled on their significant loss and demanded full and immediate restitution. Instead, they opted to place their hands in the Lord's hands and ask Him to help them forgive those who had harmed them physically and emotionally.

They truly wanted those who had harmed them to be forgiven and for the spirit of

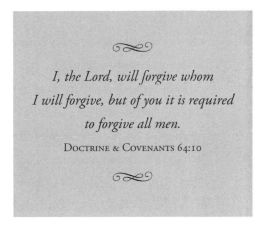

I, the Lord, will forgive whom I will forgive, but of you it is required to forgive all men.

DOCTRINE & COVENANTS 64:10

unity to be restored to their branch and community. In their righteous desires, they followed the Lord, who said, "Verily, verily, I say unto you, my servants, that inasmuch as you have forgiven one another your trespasses, even so I, the Lord, forgive you" (D&C 82:1).

Third, through adversity, the Lord blesses us with opportunities to give thanks, learn, and grow. These faithful Chilean Saints were always willing to share, and they had a vision for the work that was ignited by Elder Scott's powerful blessing to them. Through their adversity, they grew spiritually and physically. Their small branch became a solid stake, blessing the lives of hundreds of Chileans who became solid members of the Church.

They taught us that we could only realize the blessings of heaven and earth *after* the trial of our faith, *after* we do God's will, and *after* we continue in His word (see Ether 12:6; John 7:17;

8:31). Though none of us would choose to undergo adversity, we can all be spiritually strengthened through humbly seeking the Lord in times of real need.

Perhaps your family has its own hardship story that underscores the importance of seeking the Lord. It might be a story about hard work or perseverance. It might include values and principles learned by your family. Your experiences are worth recording. Don't worry about how to begin. Just write as you would if you told the story. You will be amazed at the thoughts that come to you. Remember to teach true principles the same way you learned them.

Chapter Four

STEADFAST AND IMMOVABLE

Jan J. Zwick

Our son Scott can't stand still. He loves to wander. We have lost him in the grocery store, at Disneyland, and in the airport. We have found him having lunch with neighbors we didn't even know, petting the "polka-dot dog" (a Dalmatian) at the fire station more than three miles from our home, and talking amiably with security guards at the shopping mall. In a nutshell, he is constantly in motion, which is part of what makes the following experience so memorable.

Scott lives in Provo, Utah, where he works at a wonderful workshop that employs individuals with special needs to prepare and deliver laundry to schools and hotels. On weekends he will often spend time with us in Salt Lake City. Usually I pick him up by making a trip to Provo through frenzied Friday afternoon traffic. The upside, though, is the happy spirit that accompanies us as Scott enthusiastically talks about his week as we travel back to Salt Lake City.

Because of a doctor's appointment one Friday in February several years ago, I was unable to drive to Provo. We called Scott and asked him to take the bus, which he had done many times before. But on this occasion he was to get off at a different location. I said to Scott, "Don't worry; we will be there for you. Don't wander. It is very important to stay exactly where you get off the bus." An assistant from his work drove him to the bus stop and dropped him off with a note to the bus driver indicating the stop where Scott was to get off.

Scott waited with his suitcase for the express bus to Salt Lake City. Unbeknownst to us or to his assistant, there were actually two express buses to Salt Lake City that left twenty-five minutes apart. Scott had arrived a little early and, not knowing there was another bus, climbed on the first one.

At 6:00 P.M. we arrived at the bus stop in Salt Lake City and waited. The bus arrived on time, but Scott did not get off. We thought that perhaps he had fallen asleep, so we walked through the bus looking for him. The driver had not seen anyone matching Scott's description. We called the assistant, and he assured us that he had left Scott with a note in hand in plenty of time for the bus to arrive. Well, we did what any good parent would do. We first panicked and then prayed. It began to snow, and the wind was blowing, which forced cold tears down our cheeks. We waited for the next bus to arrive from Provo. Still no Scott.

We began driving south to look at all the bus stops along the route. It was now dark, and our hearts were anxious. Here was a young man with special needs who can't read, who loves to wander, and who enjoys talking to strangers. Something occurred to us then: one of the bus drivers would have seen Scott. We went to the main bus dispatch office and gave a description of him, which went out over the radio to all bus drivers. We waited again, suspended in our own pocket of time. Finally, a call came in. A bus driver did remember Scott and that Scott had given him a note. He said that when he arrived at the bus stop, there had been an accident with a great deal of congestion. As a result, he pulled ahead one block and left Scott on the corner.

Our hearts soared.

We piled into our car and, with a police car leading us, sped to the location. What I saw that night as we came around the corner has remained a part of me ever since. There stood Scott like a towering lighthouse in a sea of darkness. His silhouette was etched against the gray night sky as large white snowflakes fell all around him. Following our instructions, he hadn't moved six inches in three hours!

We jumped out of the car and gave him a hug, marveling at the courage and obedience of this trusting young man. A scripture from the Book of Mormon came into my mind: "For they were firm, and steadfast, and immovable, willing with all diligence to keep the commandments of the Lord" (3 Nephi 6:14).

Jesus is constantly trying to say to each of us exactly what I said to Scott before he got on the bus: "Don't worry; we will be there for you." We can't wander. We must be strong, firm, and steadfast.

As King Benjamin told his people, "Therefore, I would that ye should be steadfast and immovable, always abounding in good works, that Christ, the Lord God Omnipotent, may seal you his, that you may be brought to heaven, that ye may have everlasting salvation and eternal life" (Mosiah 5:15).

For us, this experience was a metaphor for becoming anchored in Jesus Christ. In our family, Scott's determination and steadfast example helped us more clearly understand the importance of having a sure foundation. He reminded us of the benefits of steadiness and consistency in our spiritual development and progress. This simple story beautifully illustrates what it means to be solid, immovable, and firmly fixed in our obedience to the commandments and principles of the gospel of Jesus Christ. If we are faithful, we will build our life upon the foundation of the gospel of Jesus Christ rather than upon the drifting sands of man's wisdom.

We all have stories. Some of our stories are about adventures, awards, or good deeds. Some are about family heroes. They can be funny or sad. They can be about gratitude or about the Lord's intervention on our behalf. The most important thing to remember is that our experiences can build faith and link our family together.

Thank you, Scott, for teaching us to be steadfast and immovable.

I would that ye should be steadfast and immovable, always abounding in good works, that Christ, the Lord God Omnipotent, may seal you his, that you may be brought to heaven, that ye may have everlasting salvation and eternal life.

MOSIAH 5:15

Chapter Five

BUILT UPON THE ROCK

W. Craig Zwick

When I was a very young boy, my father would take me out onto large construction sites he supervised. He loved what he did, and he gave me a pure example to follow. I grew up loving the sound and movement of heavy equipment at work and of watching large buildings come out of the ground and turn into magnificent, lasting structures.

During my teenage years I enjoyed working with steel, concrete, and lumber as well as with detailed project schedules and intricate working drawings. I loved laying out buildings in the field and enjoyed every aspect of the work. The desire to create and build was such a significant part of my youth that it never left me. It was also a joy to work with my father for more than twenty years and to learn at his side as we worked closely together.

As a young priest in the Aaronic Priesthood, I remember

being out on a large project where my responsibility for an entire summer was to bring in engineered fill dirt and compact the soil for the foundation of a new school. My job wasn't glamorous, but I took the task seriously. To achieve the necessary density for the ground to support the building required just the right amount of moisture and compaction. It was repetitive work, but a solid base had to be established if the new school building was going to be properly supported—something the crusty old project superintendent constantly reminded me of. He told me that if I didn't do my job right, the building would not have a solid foundation. That was a fundamental lesson I learned early in my career in the construction business: solid buildings need to be built on solid ground.

Many years later our company was asked to build a multi-story project in Salt Lake City on a site located directly above the Wasatch Fault. The project's proximity to the fault required sophisticated and well-calculated structural engineering to build a foundation that could withstand the severe seismic conditions that an active fault might produce.

I was cautious and even reluctant to move ahead with the project because of the liability that could result from a failure in the foundation. I expressed my concern to the architect and his structural engineer.

I was assured by a very conservative and professional team that the foundation would not fail provided it was built in

Remember that it is upon the rock of our Redeemer, who is Christ, the Son of God, that ye must build your foundation . . . , which is a sure foundation, a foundation whereon if men build they cannot fall.

HELAMAN 5:12

accordance with plans and specifications. We moved ahead with the project, which included an expensive foundation system.

The foundation for this twelve-story building was designed for the highest level of safety in the event of an earthquake. It was the most elaborate and detailed foundation I had ever seen, but it was required because of the stress that would occur should the fault ever slip.

The design of the building included a three-level concrete parking structure and an additional nine floors of suspended concrete decks, concrete columns, and concrete beams. You might think that to make this building stronger you would need to increase and reinforce the mass of the entire building, but in reality, the only way to strengthen it was to strengthen the foundation.

In fact, the volume of concrete and steel in the foundation of this building was three times the amount of concrete and steel used in the entire twelve stories above the foundation.

The lesson was powerful to me. A "sure foundation" (Helaman 5:12) is vitally important if a building is to take on and survive the stress caused by earthquake, wind, or unexpected loading. In like manner we must build our lives upon a sure foundation. That is the only way to withstand the trials and temptations of life. No earthshaking challenge, doubt, fear, or spiritual tremor of any magnitude can destroy us if our foundation is built upon the rock of our Redeemer, Jesus Christ.

As Helaman told his sons, "Remember that it is upon the rock of our Redeemer, who is Christ, the Son of God, that ye must build your foundation . . . , which is a sure foundation, a foundation whereon if men build they cannot fall" (Helaman 5:12).

Our own solid foundation built on a testimony of Jesus Christ can come in unexpected ways. I can testify of this from my own experience. The year was 1967. I could feel the sunlight more than I could see it as I opened my eyes and looked through the cracks between the slats of the railroad car in which my companion, Elder Dyer, and I had been traveling all night. The rail car resembled the one portrayed in the movie *Butch Cassidy and the Sundance Kid,* and we were sharing it with two horses. Our horses. We had purchased them in Salta, Argentina, and affectionately named them Nephi and Abraham. Though our mission was the Argentina North Mission, our mission president, Richard G. Scott, had assigned us to open the work in southern Bolivia. The horses would be our transportation.

As I listened to the rumble of the train on the tracks, I

hoped that we would soon arrive. I had been serving in Córdoba, Argentina, and had barely adjusted to the bustle and confusion of that heavily populated city. I wondered what this new experience would hold for me.

The train slowed, and we finally arrived. The rustic border towns of La Quiaca and Villazón were the first indication that life in Bolivia would be significantly different from what we had known in Argentina.

The villages were located in the valley of the San Juan de Oro River. *De oro* means "of gold," which seemed such a misnomer for the area and its dusty, sleepy little villages. We looked about and could see only rock, sagebrush, red sand, and one looming ridge after another—all swept by constant wind.

Elder Dyer and I had been assigned to work in the villages of Quiriza, Chacopampa, and Chifloca, which were located about fifty miles from the border, with several rivers to cross to get there.

We came to the first river. It raced dark brown, lashing at its banks and charging like a runaway bull. I had ridden many horses before my mission, but nothing had prepared me for this. Elder Dyer instructed me to hold on to my horse's tail and swim right next to it. I resisted my reflex to kick my legs, and before long we had reached the other side.

This was the beginning of a fifteen-month experience that would help me develop my own sure foundation.

President Scott had given us specific assignments. We were

to secure a site and build a simple meetinghouse in Quiriza. We were to "establish the Church" among a beautiful and humble people. They reminded me of the people of Zarahemla in the Book of Mormon, who had become converted to the gospel of Jesus Christ because they were willing to learn and believe what they were hearing for the first time.

We came to love the Bolivian people, who were in desperate need of spiritual direction. We were unable to baptize anyone for the first eleven months of our service there because of their addiction to chicha, a highly alcoholic corn liquor that killed the amoebic bacteria from the polluted river, their only source of drinking water. It was so difficult to watch mothers lose their little children to amoebic dysentery as soon as they stopped breast-feeding.

The people were also addicted to coca, a stimulating drug that numbed their digestive systems, dampened their appetites, and gave them a short burst of energy, which allowed them to work tirelessly on few nutrients. The result was a life as beasts of burden without purpose or incentives beyond mere existence.

Part of the solution came when we taught them to build filtering systems that would provide pure drinking water. We taught them to use corn for things other than corn liquor. And, most importantly, we taught them to pray.

We taught them in their homes by candlelight. We worked alongside them in their fields, and we worked alongside them to construct a chapel in Quiriza. We felt overwhelmed by the amount of work before us, and we felt overwhelmed by the level of trust placed in us by our mission president. We felt that the work to accomplish was so much greater than our combined capacity, but we also trusted the Lord to qualify us as we obediently served Him and as we sought His guidance in each step we took. My testimony grew as a result.

I soon learned that the construction of our chapel would be different from any other construction project with which I was familiar before my mission. I felt blessed to know how to lay out a building and how to frame in wood and steel, thanks to the wise guidance and example of my father. But I felt totally unprepared to undertake a construction project in a remote village where there were no supplies beyond the natural resources of clay dirt, straw, and water needed to fabricate adobe bricks. With help from local people, we made simple molds, mixed dirt and straw, cured adobes for thirty days, and stacked them on site.

The challenges we faced in getting other needed building supplies to Quiriza were tremendous. We had to travel over a twenty-mile mountain pass called a *deshecho*—meaning it was an unfinished trail—to the neighboring city of Tupiza. On one particular trip, we rented twelve burros that we outfitted with wooden carriers we had made. We attached the carriers to the burros like saddles to carry lumber, cement, steel beams, metal decking, and millwork. The trip normally took five to six hours each way by horseback, but we knew it would take much longer because we were walking and herding the burros.

On our return trip, as we ascended the switchback trail toward Quiriza, dark, ominous clouds lumbered across the skyline. No problem. We would simply get wet. It soon began to rain. Despite the weather we pressed on, working our way along the trail. The rain intensified, and the trail became slippery. The river below us was transformed into a muddy torrent. The sound of submerged rocks being swept along clashed with the sound of the river's unrestrained fury. We pushed on. During those long hours my legs and arms ached, and I was covered with bruises and scrapes. I grew weary, and the burros began slipping. We went slowly. We knew too well what a misstep would mean.

Then one of the burros stumbled. Before we could steady him, he slid off the cliff. He crashed and tumbled, taking cement and lumber and part of the landscape with him, into the swollen San Juan de Oro River below. Inching our way to the edge of the cliff, we looked down and saw nothing but the raging river. We felt trapped on a hopeless, endless course. We sank to our knees. In that moment of desperation, I felt the Savior's presence. He became our sure foundation.

Thus sustained, we reached Quiriza safely, and work on the chapel continued. The adobe walls began to rise from the concrete foundation, and the windows were put in place. The next challenge was to place a ridge beam on the top of the gabled

adobe walls. This was a beam of eucalyptus wood, measured to fit the length of the chapel and strong enough to support the roof and the metal decking that would be installed over the wooden support structure. Placing the heavy eucalyptus beam, which weighed approximately three thousand pounds, required twenty men using woven llama-hair ropes. Men above put the heavy beam into place as men below hoisted and pulled. It was a truly a miracle that this beam made its way to the top of the building because each llama rope could support only two hundred pounds.

As the men hoisted the beam, we noticed a dangling, unmanned llama-hair rope. After the beam was lowered into its resting haunch and was firmly in place, one of our Bolivian brothers looked to heaven and then at the unmanned rope. He exclaimed, "That is the rope God held to lift this heavy beam into place on top of His chapel."

This simple but beautiful chapel stands as a sentinel over the magnificent valley of the San Juan de Oro River. It was the first Church-owned chapel completed and occupied in all of Bolivia, and it established a lasting foundation for the Church's continued growth and development throughout Bolivia.

Therefore, what? From these experiences in my early life, I learned that foundations are essential and they need to be placed on a solid base. Such foundations are the result of hard work and sacrifice and often of trial and tribulation. My sure knowledge that Jesus Christ is the Savior and the Redeemer of the world has provided me with the courage and strength to withstand the challenges I have had to face. My testimony, obtained a long time ago in the dusty little villages of Bolivia, has grown "line upon line, precept upon precept" (2 Nephi 28:30). It continues to grow today.

Take the opportunity *today* to write down or share with your family an experience that strengthened your testimony. It may be as simple as walking along a beach or listening to a talk in sacrament meeting. Don't worry about the words; concentrate on your feelings and what the Spirit teaches you.

Chapter Six

EVERYTHING TO DO
WITH THE SPIRIT

Jan J. Zwick

Sharing two experiences will allow me to convey some personal views on hearkening to the Spirit and on the profound influence the Holy Ghost can have in our lives.

Several years ago my husband and I were in New York City for a mission tour. It is always a rewarding experience to be with humble and dedicated missionaries. After a zone conference, two missionaries told us about an experience they had had the previous evening. They had been working in an area all day in the upper west side of Manhattan. The temperature was near freezing, it was getting late, and they were eager to get back to their apartment. But then they both had an impression that they needed to see someone. They obediently followed the promptings of the Spirit.

On the third floor of an imposing old building, they noticed a woman standing by the window, so they climbed the stairs and knocked on her door. A young woman opened the door, and before they could introduce themselves, she said, "I know who you are. Please come in." She told them she was Sister Pérez, a member of the Church from Puerto Rico who had recently been less active. She had served a full-time mission in Chile, had married, and had had two children. Then her husband left her. She was struggling emotionally, financially, and spiritually.

Sister Pérez then went to the table and picked up an *Ensign* magazine. She opened it to the photos of the General Authorities, pointed to a picture of my husband, and said, "Elder Zwick was my mission president. I would love to talk to him." The missionaries told her, "We are having a zone conference tomorrow, and it just so happens that Elder Zwick will be with us."

Then everything went quiet. Sister Pérez sat looking at the photo of her mission president with tears running down her cheeks. After a few moments, she asked the elders to give her love to President Zwick and me.

After the zone conference, we had dinner with two stake presidents and the mission president. We were to leave early the next morning. During the dinner, my husband and I were both thinking of Sister Pérez. My husband kept getting a prompting that said, "You should go now." We excused ourselves and traveled with the mission president across town to the upper west side of Manhattan. We arrived at Sister Pérez's apartment rather late, but still feeling the promptings of the Spirit, we knocked on her door. The door flew open and Sister Pérez fell into our arms. Through her sobs she looked at my husband and said, "President, I knew you would come."

The eighteen intervening years seemed to fade away, and we shared with one of our dear sisters a sacred experience that blessed her life as well as ours.

What if we hadn't gone? What if the elders hadn't responded to the prompting? This experience isn't about the missionaries or about us. It is about the Spirit and the guidance it provides. It is about a loving Heavenly Father blessing the life of one of His precious daughters through the Holy Spirit.

The second experience began in Santiago, Chile, in 1989. We love Chile. With its abundance and natural beauty, it offers a visual feast of rich farmlands, a crush of color, and neatly stacked vegetables and fruit along the Pan American Highway. The only thing more magnificent than the meteoric rise of the Andes Mountains is the people themselves. We love them for their heart and courage and for their faith and commitment.

Mostly I love Chile because of what I learned while we were there. Living among and serving the people, I had defining experiences that helped me progress, stretch, and grow. One of the most sacred and meaningful moments of my life came in Chile when, on my knees and with a heavy heart, I poured out my soul to my Heavenly Father and received some of the most precious, specific, and personal direction one could hope to obtain.

We had been in the mission field for only about six months, and our children were thriving—at least we thought so. They were busy with going to school, teaching with the missionaries, and learning to speak Spanish. Life, however, was a little different for Scott. He always has a happy demeanor, and so we hadn't grasped what was going on beneath the surface. Because of his disabilities, it was difficult for him to understand or speak Spanish. Conversations are his lifeline, and without the ability to converse, he was losing his happy outlook.

For security reasons, Scott couldn't leave the mission home unless he was with someone. He felt as though he was in prison. His comfort zone had been invaded. Little by little, his anxiety level escalated. We were going about our busy and demanding schedules not really comprehending what was going on inside our beloved son.

One Tuesday afternoon I was grocery shopping for the mountain of food needed to feed fifteen newly arriving missionaries. My husband was about eight hours away in the southern part of our mission interviewing missionaries. Cell phones were a thing of the future; in fact, the only phones available in the southern part of our mission were pay phones found in little obscure kiosks along the highway. We had difficulty communicating with each other when he was traveling. I returned to the mission home after shopping only to be met by three hysterical children and two distraught and concerned missionaries.

When I was finally able to make sense of their individual accounts, I felt my knees buckle and my heart stop. It seems that Scott had reached his breaking point. Because of his frustration and inability to express his feelings, he had become violent and started throwing things. Our daughter, who was sixteen, called the missionaries who were working in the office. They were unsure what to do, and they couldn't reach me. They called a doctor they knew—a psychiatrist. He arrived with two colleagues at the mission home to find Scott out of control. The doctor didn't speak English, and Scott spoke no Spanish, which only aggravated the problem. So without any discussion, they restrained Scott and took him away.

I jumped into the mission van with the address of the hospital and began negotiating the chaos of Santiago traffic, praying as I went. I foolishly thought I could drive right to the psychiatric hospital where they had taken him. "No Entry" signs and one-way streets conspired to slow my progress. I arrived at the hospital exhausted and was overwhelmed by what I saw. Conjure in your mind a dark, austere, ancient building with bars on every window. I was told I would not be allowed to see my son for at least twenty-four hours. It was the law. Imagine the emotions I felt. My heart ached for Scott. I knew he would be upset and confused, and I had no way of comforting him.

I returned to the mission home, where I spent hours fervently pleading for the Lord's help. I prayed for this trial to be taken away from me. But gradually I started to feel the Holy Ghost in great measure. The Spirit began to teach me in a voice I could not hear but could feel. I was given specific counsel borne of the Holy Ghost. I felt strongly that I was to get Scott out of that hospital as soon as possible. I knew I would soon hear from my husband, who was still in a remote part of our mission, but I also knew we must act as prompted by the Spirit.

With the help of two valiant missionaries whom I love with my whole heart, we went back to the hospital. I really didn't have a plan once we arrived but relied on the Spirit to guide me. A different receptionist who apparently didn't know the rules was at the front desk and let us in. We found Scott in a room. He was alone and had been given so much medication that he was incoherent. He had fallen and had a huge gash on his elbow, which had bled all over his bed. He was also having difficulty breathing. I went to look for a nurse. I could find no one—not in the halls or in any other room. I looked at the elders, and we knew what we needed to do. The three of us carried Scott right out the front door and into the mission van. We traveled quickly toward the mission home and safe refuge. The healing balm of those emotional and painful moments was in knowing that the Savior knew and felt what I was feeling.

This story illustrates how important I think the Spirit is in our lives and how frightening life can be without it. Through the Spirit and the prayers of family, missionaries, and faithful Saints in Chile, we saw many miracles.

I took Scott back to Utah, and his happy spirit returned. He recognized the comfort of home and family. During the next two and a half years, while we were completing our mission, Scott lived in a group home in Spanish Fork where he learned amazing skills, developed wonderful friendships, and spent time with extended family members whose love and tender care nurtured him. He progressed and grew. Again, we were guided by the Spirit to be sensitive to his needs and to know what was best for him. Our many prayers had been answered.

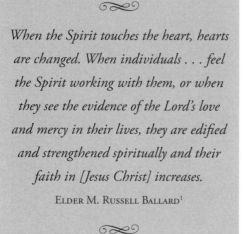

When the Spirit touches the heart, hearts are changed. When individuals . . . feel the Spirit working with them, or when they see the evidence of the Lord's love and mercy in their lives, they are edified and strengthened spiritually and their faith in [Jesus Christ] increases.

ELDER M. RUSSELL BALLARD[1]

Even today, more than two decades later, we are guided by the Spirit to know what to do for Scott and how to do it. If we hearken to the Holy Ghost, He will prompt us. He will bring peace to our souls and understanding to our minds.

The application and implementation of our stories is simple and is found in the Book of Mormon: "The Holy Ghost . . . will show unto you all things what ye should do" (2 Nephi 32:5).

I learned that amid the many noises and clamoring messengers in the world today, we must learn to recognize the whisperings of the Holy Ghost. There is no other way to gain a testimony but through the witness of the Holy Ghost. I testify we can rely on the Holy Ghost with total trust, for "when the Comforter is come, whom I will send unto you from the Father, even the Spirit of truth, which proceedeth from the Father, he shall testify of me" (John 15:26). When we live under the influence of the Holy Ghost, our testimonies will grow, and we will be consistently guided in *all* aspects of our lives.

> *Personal stories are gifts, given to us by others, stories that stay with us forever, continuing to feed and teach and inspire us.*
>
> VIRGINIA H. PEARCE[2]

Chapter Seven

LISTENING

W. Craig Zwick

Many years ago I discovered the singular beauty of Utah's Wasatch Mountains. They are beautiful in the summer for hiking and mountain biking, but in the winter they turn into a captivating brilliance of white powder snow. I could never tire of those mountain peaks that are so close to Salt Lake City. Mount Superior, Albion Basin, Peruvian Ridge, High Rustlers, Mineral Basin, Mount Baldy, Collins, and Germania are all names that bring an instant smile to my face and remind me that they are God's creations to be enjoyed with wisdom and good judgment.

I never tire of the deep and the steep. As a young boy growing up in the shadows of these peaks, I wasn't captivated just by their visual magnificence; it was the blow-away powder snow that would draw me there and keep me coming back. Every Saturday morning from mid-November to March, my friends and I would juggle our skis and sack lunches and climb on a bus for a glorious day of *schussing* down groomed and ungroomed runs in Big and Little Cottonwood Canyons at the ski resorts of Alta, Snowbird, Solitude, and Brighton.

Later in life, with more demands on my time, I became more selective regarding which days I would ski. My love for the mountains was just as strong, but my priorities and responsibilities had changed somewhat. I would wait for the perfect snowstorm so I could ski in fresh, deep, untracked powder snow. The depth of the powder snow allowed me to face straight down the mountain and seek "first tracks" in the untouched pure powder slopes of the Wasatch. The steep chutes bordered by rock outcroppings and rugged cliffs certainly increased the depth of my admiration for God's creations and for all they meant in storing living water for the warmer days of spring and summer.

Growing older, I also found myself becoming more cautious of both the conditions and the terrain. I learned to respect the powerful rush of snow in an avalanche and always carried a transponder in the event of being caught in a slide. I learned that these magnificent peaks and open bowls of snow could become treacherous with high wind and storms that could create a total whiteout in minutes, making it impossible to see and occasionally creating a serious case of vertigo.

It wasn't until years later, while traveling in the Canadian Rockies during the winter of 1988, that I learned a whole new level of respect for the terrain that had brought me so much happiness in earlier years. Jan and I had gone to Banff, Canada, to experience the Calgary Winter Olympics with some dear friends. We loved the spectacular beauty of Lake Louise and of the Canadian peaks in the Monashee, Purcell, and Selkirk mountains.

I was able to ski many of those pristine areas by helicopter, and it was exhilarating. The vertical drop and the conditions were ideal, and we relished our days in that scenic and popular skiing mecca.

On one memorable day we left early in the morning from a heliport in Canmore, Alberta, just outside Banff National Park. Our pilot and our mountain guide were the very best. They both had thousands of hours in the air and in the mountain ranges of the Purcells.

On this particular day we went prepared with sufficient food and fuel for the entire day and beyond, but our plan was to return to Banff that same February evening. Six very experienced skiers, a fine helicopter pilot, the finest jet helicopter available, and a very experienced mountain guide left in the dark of the morning for our first ascent to the peaks and bowls of the Canadian Rockies.

We were subdued and respectful as we made our initial climb out of the beautiful Banff National Park and found ourselves surrounded by nothing but white jagged peaks and beautiful open powder bowls. We had timed our skiing perfectly! We knew we were in for a very memorable day of open powder skiing, and we were thrilled and humbled to witness such indescribable beauty.

The first drop on a peak was exhilarating. As the chopper hovered just barely off the snow, we six skiers and our guide made our way onto the cornice, where we would take our first plunge down into the white face of powder snow. It was euphoric and so completely breathtaking to be making effortless turns in bottomless powder snow. I experienced such a wonderful feeling that I will never forget offering a prayer of thanks for such a splendid morning in God's creations.

Each of our eight beautiful drops of more than 2,500 vertical feet was unforgettable. We were having such a wonderful time that we did not want to stop. But fatigue was taking its toll, and our bodies were telling us it was time to take a break.

We settled into a beautiful valley surrounded by huge fir trees, and seated inside our Bell Ranger Helicopter, we felt very comfortable. We did not sense any imminent danger.

Within thirty minutes of settling in our restful spot, however, heavy cloud cover quickly moved in. Suddenly big, beautiful flakes were coming down at a rate of about four inches per hour. Within minutes, the helicopter was covered. Our pilot, Jed, said the unexpected change in weather genuinely concerned him.

He thought we should put protective canvas covers on the blades and wait out the storm. But he also realized that the storm could continue for hours, and he was concerned about the helicopter icing up. We faced a total whiteout at ten thousand feet above sea level and snow covering us at a rapid rate. The only contact we had with the outside world was by FM radio, which other aircraft would receive as an SOS. As darkness settled in, I knew that my wife and the wives of the other seven men would be concerned that we had not returned to Canmore as planned. I also knew my wife well enough to know that within another hour she would be joining the first dogsled team to go out looking for us.

Under Jed's capable command, we decided we would make one attempt to climb out of the storm. We had sufficient fuel and plenty of power to do it. The only problem was the zero visibility. The snowfall had turned everything white, and we could not see six feet in any direction. It was quiet, but our hearts were pounding loudly.

We prayed that the equipment would function well and that the elements would be calmed. We prayed that our wives would be comforted in the event we were unable to get out of the mountains that night. We prayed that we would be alert to danger and that we would be united in our efforts.

Jed suggested that the sounds outside the chopper would be our protection. Our task was to listen carefully for danger.

We removed both large doors and stowed them behind the seats, leaving the helicopter wide open. That way we would be able to hear the air beat off rock or trees if we got too close to them, alerting us to danger. We dropped a thick rope with a heavy weight attached so we could watch and listen for it to touch anything below the craft. It was difficult to listen because of the noise of the helicopter, but we listened intently with our ears as well as our hearts.

All went well, and within forty minutes we were safely on the ground in Canmore. We were grateful and expressed that gratitude in a humble prayer of thanksgiving.

Just as we had tried to listen for the sound of passing air over the roar of the helicopter, I have learned that we must listen for the voice of the Spirit over the noises and distractions of the world. Just as we had taken off both doors of the helicopter, we must rid ourselves of anything in our lives that detracts from our ability to hear the whispering of the Spirit.

Sometimes we need only do something simple such as turning off the radio, television, computer, or cell phone. Other times we need to get rid of spiritual interference caused by contention, gossip, criticism, materialism, dishonesty, or impurity in our lives. Remember, the voice of the Spirit can be both still and small (see D&C 85:6), being discerned only with great effort.

My grandchildren love to hear this story. When I conclude telling it, I usually ask them what they learned. On one occasion, five-year-old Joey said, "Grandpa, I learned that I don't want to ride in a helicopter unless they take the doors off!"

Chapter Eight

MAGNIFY YOUR CALLING

W. Craig Zwick

Our four memorable years in Brazil while I served in the Brazil Area Presidency provided many valuable lessons about the nature of true discipleship. Many of these lessons Sister Zwick and I learned from members of the First Presidency and Quorum of the Twelve Apostles in their visits to Brazil. We marveled time and again at their unselfish service and the depth of the love they extended to us and to the extraordinarily humble Brazilian people, who were always so beautifully hungry and thirsty to be taught.

Of eternal impact to our hearts and souls was an experience that took place in February 1996. Elder Neal A. Maxwell and his wife, Colleen, were to visit the members in the northern city of Fortaleza. They left Salt Lake City on Thursday afternoon and arrived in São Paulo early Friday morning after traveling for more than fifteen hours on an all-night, red-eye flight. We met them in the Guarulhos International Airport in São Paulo. From there we were to catch a four-hour flight to Fortaleza, where we would participate in a regional conference of the nine stakes in Fortaleza, scheduled for that Saturday and Sunday.

Elder and Sister Maxwell's spiritual energy and excitement were bracing and contagious. Everyone they saw knew they were special—from the young Brazilian returned missionaries working the United Airlines counter in the Guarulhos airport to the sweet, humble sister who was clearing tables at the airport McDonald's. They all wanted a glimpse of Elder Maxwell. He and Sister Maxwell were so engaging that they lifted every one of those precious sons and daughters of God as they smiled and said *tudo bem* ("all is well") in their best Portuguese.

Our flight to Fortaleza was comfortable but warm. We all sat in coach seats, and Sister Zwick and I learned much from observing the Maxwells' pure and unselfish acts of ministering to others along the way.

We were met in Fortaleza by an Area Seventy, the Brazil Fortaleza Mission president and his wife, and all nine stake presidents and their wives. They gave us a pleasant welcome, and they each recognized how vital this visit would be for this important part of Brazil's growing northeast area.

After a little rest in a hotel, Elder and Sister Maxwell asked that we join them for dinner and suggested that we meet in their room with our scriptures. We learned wonderful truths as we shared with each other our love for the Savior and our love for passages of scripture and treasured ideas that came to mind as we visited.

We marveled at Elder Maxwell's spiritual and physical energy, not knowing that earlier that same week, he had been diagnosed with leukemia. No one knew. But there he was, ministering with full heart and energy.

On Saturday morning we received a phone call from one of the stake presidents. He said one of his bishops had called that morning to ask a favor. He explained that the bishop told him of a faithful family in his ward whose seven-year-old son was in the hospital dying of leukemia.

The devoted bishop asked the stake president if he thought Elder Maxwell would be willing to come to the hospital sometime during the weekend to give this precious child, Jared Ammon, a blessing. I assured the stake president that I would ask Elder Maxwell if he was willing to do so.

Recognizing that this was the rainy season in Fortaleza, we knew that a trek across town through deep water and potentially unlit streets would be difficult. In addition, Saturday was a day of meetings with local leaders, including a four-hour priesthood leadership meeting. We would not get back to our hotel until after 10:00 Saturday night. We knew that Elder Maxwell was physically tired from his arduous days and nights in an airplane.

Nevertheless, I asked Elder Maxwell if he would be willing to go to the hospital to give a blessing to this young boy. His response was immediate and genuine, so unselfish in every way. Without any thought for his own comfort, his illness, or his lack of sleep two nights in a row, he said, "I will be honored to do it."

It would have been so simple to say, "Why don't we do it another day?" or "Do you think the Area Seventy and mission president could do it?" or "Elder Zwick, will you go take care of that for us?"

Instead, Elder Maxwell asked me to please convey his love to the family and assure them that he would be there later that night to give young Jared Ammon a blessing.

Elder Maxwell taught with power during the priesthood leadership meeting. Following the four-hour meeting, he patiently shook hands with the many faithful priesthood leaders who wanted to express personal thanks for his inspirational leadership and message of hope. He knew he had miles to go before he would rest, and yet he unselfishly reached out to each individual who wanted to shake his hand. It was such a selfless act of endurance, faith, and courage that it gave a new level of spiritual energy to the powerful priesthood potential in that part of Brazil.

It was searing hot and getting hotter by the moment as we made our way to the hospital, accompanied by the stake president and the mission president. Heavy rain had fallen throughout the day, and the streets were flowing with runoff and debris. We encountered power outages that eliminated much of the normal street lighting, and yet we moved ahead to the hospital.

We entered Jared's hospital room, where we found him in the arms of his fourteen-year-old sister, Reginani. Jared's parents, Antonio and Rita, who had sold the family car to pay for some of Jared's medical expenses, were unable to get to the hospital as they desired. As I recall, Elder Maxwell greeted Jared, looked into the young boy's eyes, and asked if he would like a blessing. Then, in a tender gesture, Elder Maxwell reached out his hand and temporarily removed Jared's oxygen mask so the boy could respond. Jared quietly but boldly said, "Yes, Elder Maxwell." Elder Maxwell then asked that I anoint this faithful young warrior and said he would seal the anointing.

The blessing was short, powerful, and meaningful to little Jared and his young sister. Elder Maxwell reminded Jared that his life was eternal and that he had accomplished much here by gaining a body and by living faithfully. He promised him that he would serve a mission in the days ahead. He also made it clear that all of this would be done within the Lord's time and in accordance to His will for Jared.

After the blessing, Elder Maxwell asked Jared if there might be anything else he would like him to do. Once again he gently removed the oxygen mask. Jared responded, "Yes, Elder Maxwell. Would you sing 'I Am a Child of God' for me?"

There in a hospital room on the other side of the world, an

Apostle of the Lord Jesus Christ, diagnosed with leukemia himself, tearfully sang "I Am a Child of God" for his newfound friend, Jared Ammon, and for his precious sister.

We left the hospital, having been lifted by what we had heard and felt. We returned slowly to the hotel, crossing some deep water at many intersections. The Spirit of the Lord provided each of us with a powerful witness of His will for young Jared.

Within an hour of arriving at the hotel, the stake president called to once again express deep thanks for Elder Maxwell's unselfish willingness to travel to the hospital and give Jared a blessing. He also informed us that the boy had passed away peacefully with a smile on his face.

We informed Elder Maxwell, who graciously expressed love to the Lord and to the family for allowing us this sacred privilege.

The Sunday general session of the regional conference went well. Then, rather than leaving Fortaleza for São Paulo that evening, the Maxwells moved their departure to Monday evening, allowing them to participate in the services for Jared.

The amazing thing was that Elder Maxwell seemed to take no thought for his own comfort. We knew he must have been incredibly exhausted, but he didn't show it. Instead, he was completely focused on Jared's family and their needs. We marveled as we watched this humble servant of God so beautifully magnify his sacred calling.

It was a tender thing to witness the love extended to Jared's

> *Inasmuch as ye have done it unto one of the least of these . . . ye have done it unto me.*
>
> MATTHEW 25:40

family by friends and neighbors who filled the stake center for the service. Elder and Sister Maxwell also lavished expressions of love on the family. Jared had been the fourth of nine children, and his parents were so grateful that Elder and Sister Maxwell were willing to be there beside them. "It is as if the Savior Himself were here with us, providing spiritual sustenance and assuring us of His love for us," said Jared Ammon's noble father.

Elder Maxwell shared this story in his April 1996 conference address; not until a year later did it become public knowledge that Elder Maxwell himself had been diagnosed with leukemia. Elder Maxwell's example of unselfish discipleship and his depth of faith provided added strength to this family and to all Latter-day Saints in Brazil. This visit was so important and will forever live in the hearts of all who were touched by its powerful impact.

This tender story is rich with principles and examples of faith and discipleship. We were uniquely taught what it means to be a true disciple of Jesus Christ. Elder Maxwell's example of the pure love of Christ helped us understand in a poignant way that by losing ourselves in the service of others, we receive help in melting away our own pain and disappointment.

As the Savior said in the parable of the sheep and goats, "Inasmuch as ye have done it unto one of the least of these my brethren, ye have done it unto me" (Matthew 25:40).

Elder Maxwell also showed us what it means to magnify our callings. He did more than was expected of him, and he did it with willingness, an open heart, and gratitude for the privilege of serving.

Finally, and perhaps most meaningfully, Elder Maxwell showed us an example of serving as the Master served.

As you ponder this story, you will receive your own tutoring and insight. Listen to the Spirit, for there will be powerful lessons for you in your own callings and in your own families.

Chapter Nine

Negative Painting

Jan J. Zwick

I first knew I wanted to paint while we were living in England. I was inspired by the beauty of the landscape—green rolling hills punctuated by clusters of sheep enjoying the lush grass. The springtime countryside sparkled with yellow canola literally covering all the fields.

I tried to record the quaint thatched-roof cottages with my camera but failed to capture the essence of the subtle and intricate play of light, textures, and colors. The grace of the architecture in London and the sturdiness of the many rock walls and castles also compelled me to begin painting.

I started simply with a few brushes and a beginning set of watercolor paints. Intimidated at first, I started out doing just small paintings. They were not very good, but they were more meaningful to me than the photographs I took. By the time I finished

a painting, I was so well acquainted with the scene that I could almost feel it, hear it, and smell it.

Even now, eight years later, I am still painting. I have produced no masterpieces, but my children display them on the walls of their homes just the same. I paint because I enjoy doing it with great friends who also enjoy creating. It brings deep satisfaction and fulfillment, and I continue to learn.

Let me tell you about one technique used in watercolor painting. I hope you will see the relationship of this technique to the experience I am about to share.

The technique is *negative painting*. It is painting the negative

> *Think of yourself as a stone carver, chipping away, until only the most precious lights remain.*
>
> BRENDA SWENSON[1]

space, which is the area around the *positive shape*. The interrelationship between the positive shapes and the negative spaces is an important compositional element.

The leaves in this painting are the positive shapes, and the dark colors around the leaves are the negative spaces, which help to enhance the subject and bring out the light. Now for the story.

Forty years ago my husband and I made a high-speed trip to the hospital because I was in early labor. Our baby was due in July, but it was only May. I was worried that our child would be born without all of his fingers and toes. I wondered if our baby would have lots of cute curly hair or be bald, as I was when I was a baby. I speculated that the baby would look like my husband. I never worried that something would go wrong. This was our first child, and I really had no idea what to expect. I remember the fluorescent lights in the delivery room, the discolored ceiling tiles, and the efficient movement of the nurses bustling around.

Our firstborn, Scott, entered the world quickly, but we didn't hear that remarkable first cry of a newborn baby for a while. The umbilical cord had been wrapped around his neck three times, and he had some problems getting here. So it was several long minutes before we heard the miraculous sound of life. He weighed a little more than three pounds, had no hair, and was completely beautiful.

I knew in my heart, however, that something wasn't right, but it was several months before we knew that Scott would be limited both physically and mentally. After consulting with the doctors, we began to comprehend the magnitude of his challenges. We wondered if we were up to the task of taking care of him and helping him to grow and learn. We knew it would not be easy for him or for us.

As a new mother and unsure of my new role, I struggled to comprehend what would be required of me. Would I understand and be able to minister to the special needs of a child with disabilities?

I began losing patience with myself and with others. I kept wondering, *Why did this happen to me?* I floundered in self-pity. My greatest frustrations seemed to come from my efforts to "handle it myself," or, in other words, from my failure to have faith in the Lord. This was a challenge for me—a big one. In my young life I hadn't yet experienced really difficult times. I just didn't feel up to the task.

One evening while reading the scriptures, I had a sweet moment of love and learning. I was reading in the Doctrine and Covenants when section 98, verse 3, spoke to my heart: "Therefore, he giveth this promise unto you, with an immutable covenant that they shall be fulfilled; and all things wherewith you have been afflicted shall work together for your good, and to my name's glory, saith the Lord."

Never before had one verse of scripture had such an impact. I immediately felt the power of the Spirit touch and expand my heart. I realized that until the Spirit stepped in, I had been totally ineffective on my own. During the tenderness of this time, I felt such peace and the Spirit's calming influence. From that moment on I looked forward to the experiences that awaited us—not with fear and discouragement but with hope and faith in the Lord.

For forty years now our life has been full of concern, decisions, problem solving, prescriptions, procedures, bills, evaluation forms, and sleepless nights. Through it all we have experienced miracles, not only in Scott's life but also in the lives of each member of our family. These experiences have stretched our understanding, built our character, and increased our compassion for others. We have shared lots of love, laughter, and a great deal of learning and growing. Scott has been at the center of it and has blessed our family in countless ways.

These events have changed me. I am not the same person I was when Scott was first placed in my arms. I have been stretched, tutored, and taught. Over time and through help from the Lord, I have learned everything from patience and faith to psychology. When we are in the midst of the refiner's fire, it is sometimes hard to really recognize what we are learning. But little by little in my day-to-day growth process, I was becoming refined. I became more loving, more aware, more tolerant, and, yes, smarter.

When I felt overwhelmingly weak, I was sustained by strength from the Lord. I have learned things that I couldn't have learned in any other way. I have been refined with a light that comes from the Lord Jesus Christ. The Lord can put anything right, but most often He changes hearts. My heart has felt the goodness of His word and His promises.

That brings me back to the idea of negative painting. One painter has observed, "Think of yourself as a stone carver, chipping away, until only the most precious light remains."[3]

Just as the dark is chiseled away to leave the precious light in

> *No pain that we suffer, no trial that we experience is wasted. It ministers to our education, to the development of such qualities as patience, faith, fortitude, and humility. All that we suffer and all that we endure, especially when we endure it patiently, builds up our characters, purifies our hearts, expands our souls, and makes us more tender and charitable, more worthy to be called the children of God . . . and it is through sorrow and suffering, toil and tribulation, that we gain the education that we come here to acquire and which will make us more like our Father and Mother in heaven.*
>
> ELDER ORSON F. WHITNEY[2]

a painting, so Heavenly Father was rubbing off my own rough edges and imperfections, helping me radiate light and blessed peace.

When Scott was born, I thought raising him would be one of my greatest challenges. Instead, it has become one of my greatest treasures.

We came to earth knowing that we would experience pain, trials, and other difficulties. I have learned how the Lord allows adversity to come into our lives to prove us to see whether we will abide in His covenant. Part of God's plan is our testing and growth.

I testify that there is a refining process in overcoming adversity that increases our understanding, enhances our sensitivity, and makes us more Christlike. No one is immune from trials and tribulations. Think of the challenges you have experienced or are in the process of navigating. Write down or share your own refining process. You will be amazed at what you have learned and what a bright light you are becoming!

Chapter Ten

BECOMING

W. Craig Zwick

A highlight of any mission president's experiences is the anticipation that accompanies the arrival of each group of incoming missionaries. While we served in the Chile Santiago South Mission, our arriving elders and sisters came on Tuesday morning every four weeks. This was an exciting time for the entire mission because everyone was affected.

We received incoming missionaries from their missionary training center experiences in Provo and in Santiago, Chile. The native Latin American elders and sisters would spend two weeks at the Chile MTC, where they would work on teaching techniques and other skills that would help them adjust to life as full-time missionaries. Our North American elders and sisters would come to us after spending nine weeks in the Provo MTC, where they focused on learning Spanish and on teaching in their new language.

In both MTCs, the anticipation was that each missionary would experience a major change in his or her heart and mind. No matter the years of seminary instruction, years of nurturing in a strong LDS family, mentoring of older siblings returned from missions of their own, or number of scripture chases they had won, these newly called missionaries were embarking on something far more demanding than any of them had previously attempted, and they knew it.

Some were native or nearly native speakers of Spanish; some had years of experience studying and teaching the gospel. Others were not sure why they had even accepted a call to serve a full-time mission. Some were convinced that they had been assigned to the wrong mission, and others believed they should still be in Southern California, where they knew the Lord wanted them to serve.

Some of our missionaries had left academic or athletic scholarships at prominent universities. Some knew that those scholarships would not be there for them in two years when they returned.

No matter their level of preparation or natural ability—or lack thereof—on their arrival in the Chile Santiago South Mission, each elder and sister was quite different after spending just a few days in that beautiful country.

Their individual circumstances were as varied as their physical appearance. Some had come in borrowed suits, and others had left their new pickup truck in the garage or sold it to pay for their mission. For some it was the first time they had ever dressed in a white shirt and tie, and for almost all it was the first time they had ever been so dependent on the Lord in their entire life.

Some had come against the wishes of their parents, and others had lost a parent just prior to their service. In our mission we had a son and a daughter of mission presidents then serving, and we had seven sons of my former missionary companions and close associates from my first mission in the Argentina North Mission.

All the missionaries were unique and had their own stories. Most of them, however, found it more emotionally wrenching to leave Chile at the end of their missions than it had been for them to leave home when they entered the MTC.

Most of our missionaries were steady and obedient. They understood the sacred purpose of their mission and were committed to the work. They also knew that they were there to serve their Master, whose name they carried on their personal name badges.

Each of our missionaries had challenges sometime during the mission. Often their very first hours in the mission—when culture shock and profound lifestyle changes were part of the new routine—were so difficult for them they would call and tell me they wanted to go home. For many it was pure and simple homesickness. Once they truly unpacked their bags and became immersed in the new lifestyle of full-time missionary service, however, they experienced a vertical acceleration of spiritual learning and started to really *become* all that their loving Heavenly Father expected them to *become*.

The amazing differences in spiritual and physical maturity among our missionaries were quite astonishing. We had Harvard graduates, and we had some who couldn't read. We had those who were fifth-generation members of the Church, and we had many who had been baptized just one year before they entered the temple and MTC on the same day. We learned important lessons from virtually every missionary. Each had a story. We came to know the purity of their hearts as a result of monthly personal interviews.

On one very rainy Tuesday morning, we received a large group of missionaries on the early morning flight into Santiago directly from Atlanta, Georgia. They had left early the day before from Salt Lake City. On this flight were ten enthusiastic elders and two fine sisters. These twelve missionaries arriving from the Provo MTC would be joined later that morning by four Chilean elders and two Chilean sisters who had completed their training in the Santiago Chile MTC.

As part of our monthly schedule, Jan and I would go to the Chile MTC, located just fifteen minutes from our home in Santiago, to pick up the new missionaries who had just completed their two weeks of training and were all very nervous to enter their field of labor. Our Chilean missionaries were normally from the outlying regions of Chile.

On this particular morning we picked up our six Chilean missionaries and brought them to the mission home to get acquainted with them and to introduce them to the twelve missionaries from North America. After enjoying a nice luncheon together, I began interviewing each of the new elders and sisters.

Among the group of elders was a young man from Puerto Montt, Chile. Puerto Montt is a beautiful city in southern Chile located on the Chilean coastline where the fishing waters of the South Pacific Ocean are hugely productive. Elder Gómez entered my office at the mission home, and I could tell he was in shock. I had learned from his brief biographical information provided by his bishop and stake president in Puerto Montt that he had been a member of the Church for exactly thirteen months.

Elder Gómez looked down at the floor and never up into my eyes. I tried to engage him in a relaxing interview, but he was so scared to be there and so afraid to open up to me or to the other missionaries that I was very concerned.

He was serious, and he knew he was in the right place; however, he harbored great fear from what he thought he did not know. He was very young in priesthood and doctrinal understanding. He was concerned that his testimony would not be adequate to teach the humble Chilean people, especially in a big city like Santiago, which was so much different from his little fishing village of Puerto Montt.

Elder Gómez shared his conversion story, and he spoke endearingly of his precious grandmother, who was the first and only other member in his family. He began to lighten up some, but he was still pensive. He said the two missionaries who had taught his grandmother and him were still serving in the Chile Osorno Mission and that they had encouraged him to serve a full-time mission. He said one of them had given him three white shirts and a suit to take on his mission. His stake president had helped him prepare for the temple by purchasing for him his first set of scriptures.

He spoke of his experiences of being out on rough seas for weeks at a time. During his periodic returns to Puerto Montt, the missionaries and his grandmother, with whom he lived, would teach him. He told me he knew that Joseph Smith was a prophet and that the gospel had been restored. He felt very good about accepting a full-time mission call from the Lord through His living prophet. As he shared these precious truths, I felt his conviction but still sensed his anxiety.

At that moment he reached into his pocket and pulled out something I neither expected nor was prepared for—a revolver. I could see that there were live rounds in the cylinder. My heart leaped to my throat. Now I was the one feeling anxiety!

He then explained that life on a ship was rough. At times disagreements would arise—along with a need to defend oneself. He said he would feel much more at peace if I would allow him to keep his gun with him. He added that he would likely not need it, but it would be his protection.

As we spoke further about the Spirit being more powerful than the sword, he started to relax. We spent more than an hour together. At the end of the interview, I had the gun and Elder Gómez was on his way with his witness of the Spirit being his defense. He would still not look up at me, however, and his self-confidence was weak.

Elder Gómez was assigned to a fine companion who was perfectly suited for him. They ultimately had rich success together, and I could tell in subsequent interviews that he was maturing nicely as a missionary and that the precious truths he was teaching others were having a positive impact on him. He became a strong and effective proselytizing missionary, and his companions loved him. He progressed each week of his mission, and at the six-month point in his service, he was ready to become a senior companion. He developed a rapport with the local leadership in each ward and stake where he served and was an obedient, hardworking missionary.

As I would see him in personal interviews each month and would accompany him on teaching appointments, I was very impressed with his spiritual depth, especially the self-confidence and leadership skills he was acquiring. His countenance no longer reflected the fears and concerns he had when he started his mission.

When Elder Gómez came into the mission home for his final interview, we met in the very same setting where he and I had first become acquainted. Now, instead of looking at the floor and being timid and afraid, Elder Gómez had replaced fear with faith. He was positive and engaging. He described the joy he had experienced as a result of his labors. It was evident he had been transformed into a capable and highly successful missionary and was a new person.

> *Individually, we need to first "follow Him," and as we do this, the Savior will bless us beyond our own capacity to become what He wants us to be. To follow Christ is to become more like Him.*
>
> PRESIDENT DIETER F. UCHTDORF[1]

To this exemplary warrior, I said, "Elder Gómez, you have really grown and developed into a powerful priesthood holder and an excellent missionary. You have been an inspirational leader in the mission, and you have progressed in every meaningful way."

This same elder who only two years earlier was afraid to say anything and was scared to be out with his first companion without the protection of his gun, looked me straight in the eye. With the powerful "sword of the Spirit" (Ephesians 6:17), he said, "President, you've progressed a lot too!"

He was right. I *had* grown and progressed. He taught me that we are all human *becomings*. He helped me understand that we do grow "line upon line, precept upon precept" (2 Nephi 28:30).

As I reflect upon this experience, I realize that I learned many valuable lessons. One lesson I learned is that there is powerful defense in the word of God. As we lift others by teaching His doctrine, we are the beneficiaries as well. We must never settle for spiritual plateaus in our progress.

We all have times when we have grown and learned something new. What are some of your experiences that have helped you become who you are today? How have those experiences increased your faith and helped you develop and expand Christlike attributes?

Chapter Eleven

SWEET BOLDNESS

Jan J. Zwick

The following story is one of our family's favorites, I suppose, for several reasons. First, it has taught us profound principles; second, it is imbued with a heartfelt and justly celebrated sense of purity.

By now you have met our son Scott several times. It is not because our other children are not as remarkable; it is just that Scott is so unpredictable and so prepared to meet the Savior. Scott has an extraordinary ability to see things as they really are, and he is so enthusiastic about life. He teaches us with his pure heart.

Scott loves to try new things. He has a great sense of adventure. When everyone else is turning up their noses at something new, such as frog legs, raw fish, and cow tongue, Scott is both willing to try it and usually likes it.

Several years ago Scott's brother Spencer invited him to

Boston for a little visit. Scott was ecstatic. Not only would he be spending time with his brother but he would also be traveling on an airplane to Boston. All by himself. The thought of the trip weighed heavily on me, but for Scott it was another adventure.

A direct flight went from Salt Lake City to Boston. With a little paperwork and some special help from the airlines, we made the arrangements. As we were driving to the airport, I quizzed Scott on everything from travel etiquette to oxygen masks—just in case.

"Okay, Mom. I know, Mom," he responded.

He boarded the plane without hesitation, basking in anticipation. And he arrived in Boston without incident.

> *The restored gospel enables you to become like Heavenly Father and Jesus Christ. The Savior has shown the way. He has set the perfect example, and He commands us to become as He is.*
>
> PREACH MY GOSPEL[1]

However, we were certain he had become well acquainted with the person sitting next to him. In my mind I could hear him exchanging greetings with every single passenger and asking questions of each one.

Then came the long-awaited rush of activities with his brother—everything from baseball games and movies to late-night conversation—and then he was home again.

But that is not the end of the story. A few days after his

return, we received an e-mail from some friends who happened to be on the same return flight as Scott. They were seated directly behind him on the plane.

They shared their feelings of awe as they watched and listened to Scott interact with other people. More important, they shared with us the conversation Scott had with the person sitting next to him on the plane. The conversation went something like this:

Scott: "Hi, my name is Scott. What is your name?"

Ben: "Ben."

Scott: "That's nice. What kind of work do you do?"

Ben: "I'm an engineer."

Scott: "That's nice. Do you like it?"

Ben: "Yes, I do."

Scott: "Well, that's nice. Where do you live?"

Ben: "Las Vegas."

Scott: "That's nice. You have a great temple there, right?"

Ben: "Yes, I believe we do."

Scott: "Ben, are you a Mormon?"

Ben: "No, but I have friends who are."

Scott: "Well, that's nice. So when are you going to join?"

Ben: "Well, I don't know. Maybe someday."

Scott: "That's nice. You will really like it. Have you read the Book of Mormon?"

Ben: "No, I haven't."

Scott: "You should because it will make you very, very happy."

What a lesson of sweet boldness for each of us! What did I learn? Volumes!

When we received the e-mail, we were so proud of our son, who can't read or write. Scott doesn't know the lessons in *Preach My Gospel.* What he does know is that the gospel of Jesus Christ makes his family happy. He wants others to feel that same joy, and he is willing and eager to share.

I thought about my own halfhearted attempts to share the gospel. I remembered the times I have sat next to someone on an airplane and, after introducing myself, taken out a book to read just to avoid the possibility of a religious discussion. How feeble is that!

Scott taught me through his pure heart that we are all disciples of Jesus Christ. I have a responsibility to spread His good news to others. I just needed to put my faith into action.

I also learned that the Lord prepares people and puts them in our path. Instead of feeling overwhelmed, unprepared, and fearful to open my mouth, I decided I was going to make some changes.

I took out my copy of *Preach My Gospel* and opened to chapter 3. I prayerfully studied the short lesson plan, the medium lesson plan, and the full lesson plan found on pages 41–43. What a treasure for each of us! The lesson is presented in a simplified manner. I became familiar and confident with these inspired pages. I am now ready for my next flight—just waiting to see whom the Lord will put in my path!

Scott, thank you for teaching me that missionary work is not passive. It is action oriented. We must be willing to do more. We have the greatest gift in the world. We need to share this glorious gift with others.

Missionary experiences contain a wealth of motivating and inspiring lessons for each of us. Think about your missionary experiences or those of your ancestors. They are priceless. Record them and share them with your children. They will be treasures that will be passed on for generations.

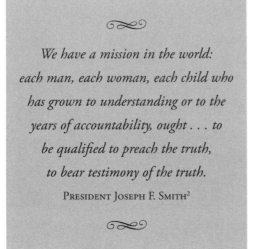

We have a mission in the world: each man, each woman, each child who has grown to understanding or to the years of accountability, ought . . . to be qualified to preach the truth, to bear testimony of the truth.

PRESIDENT JOSEPH F. SMITH[2]

Chapter Twelve

EXAMPLE, EXAMPLE, EXAMPLE

W. Craig Zwick

In my den I have an old, rough cobblestone from a street in São Paulo, Brazil. It was a gift given to me by missionaries in the Brazil São Paulo Interlagos Mission who walked and rode their bikes on those hard, rough, irregular cobblestoned streets.

The missionaries' characters, awareness, and strengths were enhanced because of their experiences traveling on those rugged granite cobblestones. My cobblestone gift is heavy and chipped and has no monetary value, but it offers me a kaleidoscope of experiences and memories.

It reminds me in its own unique way of the power possessed by solid, immovable people of integrity who, through their influence, change the lives of others. I share such a story that happened in Brazil. It demonstrates how we can gain the trust of others by living exemplary lives.

In April 1997, more than 330 elders and sisters were waiting for their visas so they could enter Brazil as full-time missionaries. Some had just received their call packet announcing their mission assignment, others were in the Provo MTC, and others had completed their MTC training and were temporarily assigned as "visa waiters" to other missions in the United States.

The visas had been delayed at the Brazilian Consulate Offices in Los Angeles, New York, and Washington, D.C., for various reasons, but one of the reasons for the delay was an old law that had recently surfaced. It stated that a religious visa would be given to North Americans only if the applicant had a bachelor's degree in religious theology from a credible university in the United States.

Of the more than five thousand American missionaries then serving throughout Brazil, not one of them had a bachelor's degree in religious theology. The Missionary Department of the Church had received clear instructions from the First Presidency and the Quorum of the Twelve Apostles that missionaries would continue to be assigned to Brazil.

At the time I was serving as the Area President of Brazil, and I felt an overwhelming responsibility to meet this serious challenge. The new missionary training center in Brazil was just being completed with a capacity of more than seven hundred missionaries. The plan was to bring our North American missionaries directly into the Brazil MTC for their premissionary training without them spending any time in Provo. The twenty-six missions throughout Brazil depended upon a steady flow of missionaries to replace those who were departing. We had the equivalent of two missions waiting for visas with no solution to fill our newly constructed Brazil MTC. How in the world were we going to fill it with this stoppage of visas?

I returned to Salt Lake City for general conference and met with Elder Russell M. Nelson. At the time he was my contact in the Quorum of the Twelve for all ecclesiastical and temporal matters in Brazil.

He directed that missionaries would continue to be assigned to Brazil even with the visa stoppage. If the problem continued, our number of missionaries waiting for religious visas would increase well beyond the 330 waiting at that time.

Elder Nelson said, "The Lord will help you solve the problem." I asked for a blessing, which lifted me and provided hope and new ideas for a solution. We arranged for a thirty-minute appointment with President Henrique Fernando Cardoso, the President of Brazil; and with the Secretary of State, Affonso Emilio de Alecncastro Massot.

We decided to prepare a presentation using graphics to show the years and many hours of preparation and training elders and sisters receive before receiving their mission calls. The presentation detailed the huge number of hours it took to complete the requirements in Primary, Young Men and Young Women, seminary, Sunday School, and institute. That cumulative time exceeded the hours, and years, it would take to receive a bachelor's degree in religious theology at any university.

We also prepared to discuss the young men and young women who had become solid goodwill ambassadors for Brazil during their years of missionary service as they came to know and love the Brazilian people and their culture. In addition, we planned to describe how LDS missions prepared young men and young women to serve as great leaders in business and in the community following their missionary service.

Brother Moroni Torgan, a returned missionary from Brazil and an influential political leader there, was asked to be my companion in this important meeting held in Brasilia, the nation's capital. Brother Torgan is a fourth-generation Latter-day Saint and was then serving as vice governor of the Brazilian state of Ceará. We had prepared well, and although my heart was racing, I felt confident that the outcome would be positive. Both Brother Torgan and I knew that the Lord knew of our dilemma and that He would not let us down in our important assignment.

I was working on two assumptions: one, that our presentation would be acceptable; and two, that the Lord was in charge.

As we were waiting to meet with President Cardoso, we received word that he had just received an unexpected visit from the president of Mexico and therefore was forced to send a substitute to our meeting. He apologized and offered to change the meeting to a later time. We decided, however, to go ahead with the meeting with Secretary of State Senhor Massot and the replacement President Cardoso would send. This man, whom we had never met previously, was Melantonio Neto, the minister of higher education.

We entered the meeting room and after some brief introductions, Minister Neto, the assigned representative of the president, said, "I know why we are here, and if it is all right with you, Senhor Massot, I would like to first tell you a story about two Mormon missionaries from America. I met them over ten years ago when they came to our home to teach my father about the Mormon church."

I struggled to maintain my composure. But then we listened in awe. Melantonio Neto continued:

"My father received all of the lessons. I was there also. We did not join the Mormon church, but I have never met two more impressive young men than those missionaries.

"They always arrived punctually. They were always clean, and their appearance was most impressive. They were courteous and respectful. They listened to my father's concerns, and they tried to help him. They had a love for our country and the people of Brazil that was so sincere they made us all feel good about everything else they shared."

Then came the bombshell! Melantonio Neto said, "From my personal experiences with these two fine missionaries, it would be my recommendation that we grant every pending visa that has been formally requested by these prospective missionaries."

I looked at my companion, whose mouth was figuratively hanging open and who was literally teetering precariously on the edge of his chair. Neither of us could speak. We hadn't said a single thing in support of our request. We hadn't even shown our graphics presentation, which was so beautifully prepared to defend the spiritual and theological preparation of each missionary for whom a visa was requested.

> *True to the faith that our parents have cherished,*
>
> *True to the truth for which martyrs have perished,*
>
> *To God's command,*
>
> *Soul, heart, and hand,*
>
> *Faithful and true we will ever stand.*
>
> HYMNS, NO. 254[1]

Senhor Massot turned to me and simply asked, "How many visas would you like?" I responded clearly, "We would like two hundred a month, sir."

Without flinching and without hesitation, Senhor Massot said, "We will assure you of sixty religious visas a week." He then told us he would send a notice that very day to the consulates in Los Angeles, New York, and Washington, D.C., to ensure that our request would be honored.

I looked across at Moroni Torgan, who looked dazed. We could scarcely believe what we had just heard.

We had not said a single word of our presentation. The consulate offices became steady in their performance, and all 330 of our missionaries waiting for visas received them within six weeks. We then continued to receive religious visas for our missionaries at a rate of about sixty a week.

Our success had nothing to do with my companion or me. It had everything to do with two outstanding missionaries who, ten years before, had obediently and diligently served. Undoubtedly, they were disappointed that the Melantonio family didn't accept the invitation to be baptized members of The Church of Jesus Christ of Latter-day Saints, and perhaps they felt they had failed. Instead, unknowingly, they had blessed an entire nation! I wish I knew the names of these two valiant missionaries who had no idea they had succeeded in ways so huge that it is difficult to measure them. I would love to thank them for their obedient and faithful service, which truly was the reason the visas were granted.

> *Paul counseled his beloved associate Timothy, "Let no man despise thy youth; but be thou an example of the believers, in word, in conversation, in charity, in spirit, in faith, in purity."*
>
> See 1 Timothy 4:12

> *What you are thunders so loudly in my ears, I cannot hear what you say.*
> RALPH WALDO EMERSON

Paul counseled his beloved associate Timothy, "Let no man despise thy youth; but be thou an example of the believers, in word, in conversation, in charity, in spirit, in faith, in purity" (1 Timothy 4:12). These two missionaries were indeed an example of the believers.

I learned two specific principles from this story:

First, there is no more powerful missionary message we can send to the world than the example of an obedient and happy Latter-day Saint. When we set solid examples of spiritual integrity, we gain the trust and respect of others. As the Lord said to Alma and the sons of Mosiah, "Go forth . . . that ye may show forth good examples unto them in me, and I will make an instrument of thee in my hands unto the salvation of many souls" (Alma 17:11).

Second, example is more powerful than precept. As parents, teachers, and leaders in God's kingdom, we must remember that Jesus Christ is the Great Exemplar to us. We are called to labor in His vineyard and to accept great responsibility. If we expect others to live up to gospel principles, standards, and ideals so they can enjoy the privileges and blessings of the gospel, then we cannot fail to maintain these requirements in our own lives.

Chapter Thirteen

TEACH BY EXAMPLE

Jan J. Zwick

Consider for a moment the important but almost unconscious things we do every day as parents. Often we don't think about our actions, but children are constantly observing and trying to emulate our example, and they often provide majestic moments in this mortal classroom.

It was Halloween and we were visiting our children and grandchildren living in California. The house was full of activity. The costume-gathering process consisted of trips to half the stores in California, and of course there were last-minute changes. We arranged forty bags of Halloween candy in bowls and containers, ready for the onslaught of trick-or-treaters. We prepared the traditional chili and cider, and I spent the afternoon with the boys making and decorating Halloween sugar cookies. Flour and candy sprinkles trailed them throughout the house. We had a good time.

I awoke early the next morning, walked into the kitchen, and noticed one remaining sugar cookie on a plate on the table. I love sugar cookies. I picked it up and was just about to stick it in my mouth before anyone saw me when our four-year-old grandson, Taylor, sleepily looked up at me. His eyes, however, were focused on the cookie. So I broke the cookie and gave half to him.

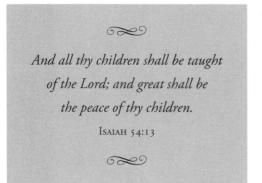

And all thy children shall be taught of the Lord; and great shall be the peace of thy children.

Isaiah 54:13

I didn't think any more about the incident until the afternoon, when Taylor came and sat on my lap. He looked up at me and said, "Grandma, you must really love me a lot."

I said, "Of course I do. You are very special to me. How do you know that I love you?"

"Well, I know because when you broke that cookie, you gave me the biggest part."

Sharing a cookie with my grandchild may have seemed insignificant to me, but to an observant and sensitive child, that little gesture was a big thing because it represented my love for him. Similarly, everything we do in life—whether good or bad, simple or profound—affects or influences someone, especially our children.

In the following two experiences, my grandchildren provided me with momentous metaphors of the extraordinary power of our examples. These stories also serve as a reminder of how our children learn by observing their parents.

Our daughter, Jen, and her husband, John, have eight active children. Their lives are occupied with eventful and time-consuming responsibilities and activities. Because they had difficulty spending time alone with each other, they elected to have a date night every Friday night. Often that date night would include a temple session.

> ᏽᎵᎬᎵᏋ
>
> *We should never permit ourselves to do anything that we are not willing to see our children do. We should set them an example that we wish them to imitate.*
>
> PRESIDENT BRIGHAM YOUNG[1]
>
> ᏽᎵᎬᎵᏋ

Because life was busy, they also determined the need to spend some one-on-one time with each of their children. So once a month, on their Friday date night, they decided to invite one of the children to do something of their choice with their parents. They selected Audrey as the first child to have this unique opportunity for an outing with Mom and Dad. She was four years old and very excited.

When Friday night finally arrived, she dressed in her best Sunday dress and then waited patiently by the door for her parents. As they walked out the door, Jen said to Audrey, "This is your special night. We can do anything you would like to do. Would you like to go to a movie or to dinner?"

Audrey stopped and then got a puzzled look on her face. "But, Mom and Dad, aren't we going to the temple?"

She had watched her parents prepare every Friday evening to go to the temple. She observed how they looked forward to that event. She watched them leave wearing their nicest clothing. She knew in her pure little heart that the temple had significant meaning to her parents. Because of her parents' pattern of regular temple attendance, Audrey had learned to cherish the temple.

The second story makes me smile. Every time I pass a McDonald's restaurant, there's no doubt that I will see in my mind's eye the excitement and illumination on my three-year-old granddaughter's chubby little face. This story is about Allie, but it really has more to do with her parents.

After an outing to the mall with three very active grandchildren under the age of four, I needed to sit down. When I suggested McDonald's for a little lunch, there was no turning back. All three of them, including the toddler, were off and running through the legs of other shoppers toward McDonald's. Sure, I should have suggested something a little more healthful, but I knew they would be happy and quiet, at least for a few minutes.

Of course, they wanted the traditional Happy Meals with chicken McNuggets and fries. As we waited in line, they jumped up and down, and I kept losing sight of the toddler. Exhausted and muttering under my breath after we had received our meals, I found a table where we could sit down. They couldn't wait to open their little boxes—not for the chicken McNuggets but for the toy that is part of every Happy Meal. Allie eagerly began plowing through her french fries as she pursued her prize.

At that time McDonald's was having a promotion of the movie *Tarzan,* and the prize in the Happy Meal was a plastic replica of Tarzan, complete with loincloth and great big muscles.

As Allie tore open the wrapping, she yelled with joy, "Look, Grandma! It's Nephi!"

Teaching is done by precept and example, and by word and deed. A good model is the best teacher.

PRESIDENT EZRA TAFT BENSON[2]

She was elated with her toy. She obviously knew about Nephi, his stature, and his characteristics.

She had been taught by loving parents that Nephi was a very important and special prophet. Parents teach most effectively by what their children see them do. Allie had observed that the scriptures were important to her parents. She had listened to scripture stories and knew that Nephi was someone significant.

How do we best teach our children? We teach by example. Good parental examples provide spiritual nourishment and build faith in our children. These two stories taught me that our children will learn far more by observing us doing righteous things than in any other way.

Simple family stories such as these define our values in subtle yet powerful ways. These experiences from our daily actions can be touchstones for our families and are laden with significance, meaning, and impact.

You don't need to be a master storyteller. Just write down some simple interactions you have had with your children or grandchildren. You will soon have a treasure trove of your own noteworthy stories that can reinforce gospel principles.

Chapter Fourteen

CHOICES

W. Craig Zwick

As a young missionary serving in the Argentina North Mission, I learned about making choices. Some choices are very important, and others are not. I came to understand that to make correct choices, an individual needs to be led by the Spirit and not by popular opinion.

The village of Quiriza, Bolivia, where I spent approximately half my time as a missionary, depended upon rainfall and a robust corn crop for survival. These humble people sustained life by using the muddy, contaminated water from the San Juan de Oro River. This river represented liquid gold to the hard-working farmers who lived along its banks and who planted their crops on small parcels of land.

We loved the beautiful Bolivian people. We loved them for their inherent goodness and for their faith, heart, and courage.

Life was hard for them. By North American standards they lived in dreadful poverty, surviving on little more than corn, beans, and the stimulating coca leaf. We helped them as best we could by installing water filtration systems that made it possible for them to get clean water and by working with them in their fields.

The residents of Quiriza and the surrounding villages planted seeds they had preserved from the previous harvest. Corn was their main crop, and we ate corn in every form possible. We had it for breakfast, lunch, and dinner. It wasn't the sweet corn you can purchase from the farmer's market; it more closely resembled the corn used for livestock feed. Nonetheless, corn, corn, and more corn was all we ate.

I remember a moment when my companion and I arrived at the little outpost where we went every two weeks to buy our supplies. The humble Bolivian who worked at the store had been waiting for us. It was rare that we could buy anything that resembled food from home, and he was excited to show us a box that had arrived from the United States. I must admit, he had our attention. As he opened the box with great fanfare, guess what we saw—twelve boxes of Kellogg's cornflakes!

Each year's harvest was important, and all depended upon the natural elements. The year we were there the people were very low on corn seed. What could we possibly do to help them plant sufficient corn for their needs?

Just about that time Richard G. Scott, our mission president, was informed that a U.S. aid to agriculture program had available a large quantity of high-grade corn seed. The only catch was that someone had to meet Dr. Allred in Tupiza, Bolivia, on a certain day at a certain time. President Scott knew how important these seeds were and decided to make the long, hard journey to get them. The trip would take him from Córdoba, Argentina, to Tupiza, passing through Tarija. The way the crow flies, it is about a day's travel, but with the rugged terrain and lack of roads, it would take a good deal more time.

I had returned to mission headquarters in Córdoba, Argentina, to accompany President Scott to Tupiza in the mission's five-year-old Jeep Gladiator. This vehicle was roadworthy, but would it handle the rugged riverbeds and elevations of southern Bolivia? We prayed it would. We drove through Argentina on asphalt pavement and then continued our journey into the rough mountain passes of Tarija, Bolivia. We planned to spend the second night of our trip in Tarija and leave early the next morning for Tupiza.

When we arrived in Tarija, however, our plans changed. We learned that a political uprising was taking place. Revolutionary Che Guevara had come to stir Tarija into a political frenzy, with his communist regime looming over the people. We were told that anyone who resembled a North American was in danger. We discussed our options with U.S. government and educational officials. They discouraged us from leaving that night and encouraged us to wait it out for a few days. President Scott listened to all of the reasons and options. We then went back to our hotel and knelt in prayer, asking for direction and answers as to what we should do. President Scott decided to leave Tarija very late that night.

We checked out of our hotel at midnight, fueled our Jeep Gladiator, and prayed for guidance. As we left the city, taking the back roads, we saw remnants of a political rally—strewn literature and propaganda covered the streets. But no one seemed to notice us, and we began our ten-hour drive to Tupiza.

We knew there would be guard stations along the way, and we relied on the Spirit to help us make the best choices. As we approached the first highway control point, we knew we would be stopped. A military guard sat in a chair with a weapon propped at his side. A heavy chain hung between two concrete bollards, blocking the roadway. I was driving the Jeep, and President Scott was carefully watching the surrounding areas.

We stopped a little distance from the guard station. For several moments President Scott said nothing. I merely sat and patiently waited. Then he turned to me and quietly said, "Go around the chain and don't stop." I followed his counsel, and we slowly drove off the road and out onto rough terrain, bypassing the guard. To our astonishment, we could see that the guard was asleep. He never looked up, and we kept going.

We knew that there would be other challenges ahead, but we

gave prayerful thanks that we had made our way out of the immediate harm's way of Tarija and Che Guevara.

After two hours of being beaten nearly to death by the wash-
board roadway, we observed that the Jeep's engine's temperature
had risen to a dangerous
level. We were in a remote
spot, with no sign of a village or water. President Scott
asked me to stop and turn off
the engine. After a prayer of
thanks for our safety thus far,
we sat quietly. Then we heard
it—rushing water. It was right
below us. We pulled off two
hubcaps and climbed down
the mountainside to the river
below. We filled the hubcaps

> *Often when we pray for help with a
> significant matter, Heavenly Father
> will give us gentle promptings that
> require us to think, exercise faith, work,
> at times struggle, then act. It is a
> step-by-step process that enables us to
> discern inspired answers.*
>
> ELDER RICHARD G. SCOTT[1]

with water and then returned to the Jeep to fill the radiator. We
made three more trips, and with each trip we gave additional
thanks.

But that was not the end of the challenges or choices we had
to make. We resumed our journey, but soon our fuel began to
run low. Again we could see no sign of life, and we had no GPS
telling us where the closest gas stations were located. It was the

middle of the night, and we needed to reach Tupiza by 7:00 the next morning.

With a wary eye on the gas gauge, we continued our journey. After a time we could see a light ahead of us. It was a tiny village, but there was no gas station in sight. As we came to the other end of the village, we observed a large truck parked near an adobe home. Four large barrels stood on the truck's open bed, and we wondered if the barrels might contain oil or fuel. It was as if the truck had been parked there just for us.

> *Should we not, therefore, continually and profoundly express to our beloved Father, as well as we are able, our unbounded gratitude for the supernal gift of prayer and for His answers that meet our needs while motivating us to grow?*
>
> ELDER RICHARD G. SCOTT[2]

Recognizing the late hour, we hesitated disturbing the people inside the house. But we had no other option. We knocked on the door and waited. No one came. We waited a little longer. Then we opened one of the barrels and could quickly tell it was fuel. We had a choice to make: we could go on and hope to find fuel somewhere else, or we could use the fuel right in front of us and leave some money to pay for it. We made the choice to use the fuel. But as we were siphoning the gas from the barrel into our gas tank, a young man came around the corner of the house and confronted us. He informed us that the truck belonged to him. When we described our dilemma, he was sympathetic and gladly accepted money for the fuel.

Daylight came just as we were approaching Tupiza, and we met Dr. Allred and his team right on time. They generously loaded our Jeep with five monster bags of corn seed. Not only was the Jeep full, but our hearts were full as well—filled to overflowing. With corn seed in the back of our Jeep, we now undertook the final twenty-mile leg of our journey into Quiriza.

Choices? Yes. Inspiration? Yes. Miracles? Yes. Blessings? Yes.

Our deep gratitude for the tender mercies of the Lord soon increased thanks to the beautiful planting and growing season that followed. Sufficient and timely rain and plentiful sunlight produced a memorable crop that was God given and exceeded any other in memory. The blessings of the harvest—along with our safety and success in obtaining the seeds—came from a loving Heavenly Father.

My mission president was a consummate teacher. In his deliberate and patient way, he would quietly seek the Lord's guidance, wait upon the Spirit, and then teach a profound lesson—either by precept or example. I could share many more examples and stories of how he taught me lessons for life. In fact, I have often said that every valuable and correct decision I have made in my life is in some way linked to President and Sister Scott and the eternal truths I learned from them on my mission.

From this particular experience with President Scott, I learned two valuable principles:

First, as we seek to receive and apply guidance in order to make good choices, we must not focus on worldly directions, popularity, or trends. We must not be influenced by popular opinion. Instead, we should be directed by the Spirit in all our choices. If we focus on doctrine and faith in the Lord Jesus Christ, we will have a totally reliable and unchanging guide for making our life's decisions.

> *And he who receiveth all things with thankfulness shall be made glorious.*
>
> DOCTRINE & COVENANTS 78:19

To make an intelligent and correct decision, we need to evaluate all available facts. But that is not enough. Making correct decisions involves prayer and the inspirational guidance of the Spirit.

Second, I learned that an expression of gratitude is an expression of faith that brings blessings. The Lord said, "And he who receiveth all things with thankfulness shall be made glorious" (D&C 78:19). As we continued to express heartfelt gratitude for each incremental bit of progress or success on our journey to get the seeds, our eyes opened to a multitude of other blessings that enabled us to succeed and to sense the divine presence that constantly protected us.

As we "pray without ceasing, and . . . give thanks in all things" (Mosiah 26:39), expressing gratitude for the direction of the Spirit and for the blessings we receive, our capacity to learn by the Spirit will increase. Expressing gratitude will also permit the Lord to guide our lives and increase our capacities.

Chapter Fifteen

I Know I Can

Jan J. Zwick

When I was a young girl living in Seattle, I looked forward to summer. Our family would travel thousands of miles in our little Nash Rambler station wagon to stay with my grandpa and grandma in Castle Dale, Utah.

Castle Dale wasn't much of a town. It had one small grocery store called a co-op, a post office, and a barbershop with one chair and a red-and-white barber pole. The only pharmacy within a fifty-mile radius was owned by my grandpa. My mom and dad had a remarkable sense of what was important and would not allow us to miss a childhood memory that decades later could not be obtained at any price. So off we would head to Castle Dale to create those memories. These trips are among my earliest memories.

During the summer, to help pay our board and room, my

sister and I would work in the drugstore. My grandpa gave me the title of manager and my sister the title of assistant manager, only because she was younger. It sounds very impressive, but it really meant that we were in charge of washing the soda fountain glasses, sweeping the sidewalk in front of the building, and taking out the trash.

It wasn't until much later, when I had a family of my own, that I realized how much I had really learned in my nonpaid position as manager of the Hunter Drug Company. I didn't recognize it at that time, but through his example and subtle guidance, my grandfather was teaching me how to work and what it means to do your best.

If I complained about my duties, which happened all too often for a manager, Grandpa would just smile and then say something that has pasted itself permanently into the center of my mind: "Jan, look for opportunity in every challenge."

I learned our family not only valued hard work and doing our best but also that courage and a positive attitude help us accomplish hard things and feel good about the tasks at hand. Grandpa's advice has blessed our entire family. We believe that with faith, courage, and enthusiasm, we can achieve!

Take Scott, our son with all kinds of disabilities, for instance. One spring he decided he wanted to participate in the Special Olympics, which were to be held at BYU's Lavell Edwards Stadium. It is a full-scale event, complete with medals and opening and closing ceremonies. For three days these special athletes take center stage and demonstrate the skills and confidence they have developed through countless hours of practice and training.

Scott was excited and had signed up to participate in three events: the 50-meter run, the 25-meter run, and the softball throw. Never mind that he hadn't thrown a softball in his life. This was a new challenge for Scott, and he went about training for it with great enthusiasm. Every day he would practice throwing the softball. There was only one problem: when Scott would throw the ball, he would hang on to it too long and end up throwing it down instead of out. No matter how hard he would try, the ball would land at his feet and dribble a few inches away. Despite his lack of ability, he kept asking me, "Mom, do you think I will win a medal?"

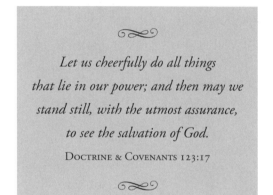

Let us cheerfully do all things that lie in our power; and then may we stand still, with the utmost assurance, to see the salvation of God.

DOCTRINE & COVENANTS 123:17

Every day Scott would put the three softballs we had bought him into a bag and go outside, where he would practice throwing them. It didn't seem to matter that he wasn't improving. He always had a smile on his face as he said, "Mom, I can't wait for the

Special Olympics." He never gave up.

Sometimes he wanted us to watch him, and other times he wanted us to pick up the balls. This went on for several months. Finally, on the day of the event, he stepped up to the line and threw the softball farther than he had ever thrown it. His throw was good enough to win him a bronze medal. You wouldn't have believed how happy and proud he was. The bright smile of satisfaction on his face probably contributed significantly to global warming!

I have learned that I really do have control to a great degree over my circumstances. If I don't like them, I've found there are certain things I can do to change them. If I want to move to higher ground, if I want to have more positive experiences, I must think about life in positive terms, not dwell on the negative.

Elder M. Russell Ballard[1]

So what did I learn? This one simple but compelling story reinforced the wisdom of Grandpa Hunter's motto: "Look for opportunity in every challenge." It also reinforced the following verse from the Doctrine and Covenants: "Let us cheerfully do all things that lie in our power; and then may we stand still, with the utmost assurance, to see the salvation of God" (D&C 123:17).

It may seem to the world that Scott isn't able to accomplish much and that his challenges limit him, but his positive attitude and desire to succeed have helped him attain many things, even beyond his normal capacity.

Because we have a knowledge of the gospel of Jesus Christ and know that we are spiritually begotten children of God, we should be the most positive-thinking people in the world. We know that our loving Father in Heaven has put us on earth to succeed, not to fail. Each of us can develop a positive attitude that will allow us to give our best effort and in doing so find happiness and success.

What did this story teach you? Perhaps you learned different principles. What are they? Maybe this story can be a catalyst for pondering your own experiences.

What thoughts came to you as you read this story? I hope you will write them down and make sense of them in any way you wish. There is no right way or wrong way. Listening to the Spirit can teach you important values through your own experiences.

Chapter Sixteen

One-on-One

W. Craig Zwick

Just as the sun was coming up on a brisk, spring morning in 1963, I headed to the stake center to meet my priests quorum adviser. It was Saturday and, oh, how I longed to be almost anywhere but digging weeds at the church. I was pretty much a normal sixteen-year-old kid, totally into myself and involved with countless activities.

The night before, my adviser had called me at home and asked me to participate in a service project. He described it as "a great opportunity to work together to improve the looks of the gardens at the church." I had made big plans to hang out with my friends, but when he said, "Craig, can I count on you?" I felt as though I didn't want to let him down. Well, the next morning, I wondered what I had been thinking. Spending my Saturday weeding a garden was like babysitting my little brother, but at least I loved my baby brother.

For you to really appreciate this story, I need to tell you about my priests quorum adviser. He and his family had recently moved into our ward. He was young and dynamic. He loved the young men and was a spiritual role model. His name was M. Russell Ballard. It would be years before he was sustained a member of the Quorum of the Twelve Apostles, but even back then he was impressive and lived close to the Spirit. He was a pure motivator of young men, and he understood each of us very well. He knew just how to get us engaged in things that really mattered.

So on that morning I arrived at 7:00 A.M. to find Brother Ballard in his work pants and baseball cap. He was alone. We had seventeen priests in our ward, and I couldn't believe I was the only one to show up.

Initially we worked side by side without saying much. I must admit that Brother Ballard knew I was a little put out, so he was patient. It wasn't long, however, before he started asking me questions. We talked about my family, my friends, and school. As we visited, the grueling job of weeding was forgotten, and Brother Ballard shifted the conversation to education, career, mission, thinking straight, and even the importance of choosing to live gospel principles.

The day wore on, and the astounding thing to me was that we had had fun. In addition, I hadn't even realized that we had weeded around the entire building!

Almost five decades later, the images of that day are still fresh in my memory. I remember how Elder Ballard made me feel. I remember some of the counsel he gave me, the smile on his face, and the genuine compliments he gave me as we completed our task and headed home.

It would be years before I would come to appreciate the true impact of that experience. Recently, Elder Ballard and I were reflecting on our experiences in the Monument Park 13th Ward. I asked him if he remembered the long day we spent pulling weeds together at the church. In what I know was a voice of annoyance, I said, "Could you believe that I was the only one of our seventeen priests who came to pull weeds that day?" I added that I felt the other young men had missed out on a great opportunity to learn from him.

He looked me straight in the eye and with a smile on his face said, "Craig, you were the only one I invited."

In my wildest dreams I could never have imagined at the time that he had singled me out to spend an entire day with me. I thought about his own young family at home without their dad. I thought about the love I had felt from him and the wise counsel he gave me. As I have contemplated his words and the impact of that event, I have been reminded again of the importance of "the one." What he did for me that day profoundly affected my life.

> *And when he had said these words, he wept, and the multitude bare record of it, and he took their little children, one by one, and blessed them, and prayed unto the Father for them.*
>
> 3 NEPHI 17:21

This story teaches many lessons, but the most important thing I gain is this: the one-on-one moment spent with caring parents, spouse, or an adult leader can be truly productive. Moments such as these are priceless, and when they become available, the opportunity must not be wasted. To be effective, these moments need not be filled with spectacular activities. Often it is quiet conversation in which genuine interest is shown that creates the powerful effect.

The Savior demonstrated his love for the Nephites through just this kind of one-on-one interaction, when "he took their little children, one by one, and blessed them, and prayed unto the Father for them" (3 Nephi 17:21). His gentle touch and tender words of prayer on behalf of every child surely spoke volumes about His love for each of them and His empathic understanding of each one's unique personality, experiences, and challenges.

It was an important time in my life, a time when a young person can incline toward the Lord or away from Him. Elder

Ballard was a true shepherd watching out for his flock. His love and sound counsel reinforced my desire to do what was right. For that I will forever be grateful to a caring priests adviser and eternal friend, Elder M. Russell Ballard.

Chapter Seventeen

LOVE ONE ANOTHER

Jan J. Zwick

We had just left the mind-boggling traffic and endless rubble of Cairo, Egypt, and were bumping along a dirt road in an ancient van through an expansive desert. Coming from the chaos and blaring noises of Cairo, we were immediately struck by the stunning silence of the desert. For all their desolation, deserts live, breathe, and teach. In that desert I gained tremendous insights that have remained with me ever since.

My husband was serving in the Area Presidency of the Europe Central Area, and we had been assigned to visit LDS humanitarian missionaries serving in the Middle East. We were on our way to a project that a senior missionary couple had been supervising. This particular project was a sophisticated water-filtering system the Church had installed to purify water coming directly from the Nile River to a leper colony and a nearby village.

This leper colony was in the middle of the desert. The lepers did not live there by choice. They had been forced into this wilderness and isolation because of fear and attendant persecution. Nine hundred men lived in this colony. About two kilometers (a little more than a mile) away was a village of about four thousand relatives, all outcasts from society.

I have unspeakable gratitude for what I learned in the desert that day. I learned that deserts could have scorching days and freezing nights, sand and rocks, total silence of vast empty spaces, and sandstorms that can fill everything with grit and bury a tent in an hour. In the desert there is no rhythm of the seasons, no rise and fall of the sap, but rather an empty wasteland where only the varying temperature marks the passage of a year. I learned that living in such a setting causes people to view things from a different perspective. That is the stark environment where those unfortunate people were trying to survive.

Finally, and perhaps more meaningfully, I came to know that there was more to this place than the eye could see. In the desperate circumstances in which these afflicted souls were living, remarkable and caring people had set their own comfort and safety aside to minister to those who had contracted the cruel and misunderstood disease of leprosy. The stories of those humanitarians were beyond belief and totally inspiring.

When we arrived, we were greeted by a wonderful senior couple from southern Utah. They had been serving for about six months. We learned that this was their second mission. Every day they traveled more than an hour to direct the work being done to build a water purification system so hundreds of afflicted people might have clean water to drink.

This selfless couple also worked in the village, where they taught English to the children and instructed the women on the use of donated sewing machines. They were busy from dawn until dark. But that is not the image that is still vivid in our memories.

The couple absolutely loved what they were doing, and you could see it in their eyes. I watched in awe as the sister missionary tenderly put her arm around one of the men in the leper colony. His face looked as though it might have been an illustration on a brochure warning against skin cancer. He wore a long brown robe, the kind you would imagine was worn when Jesus was on the earth. His hand had been amputated and was only a stump with open sores. He was wearing leather sacks on his feet.

This sweet sister said with a smile and genuine concern on her face, "How are you feeling today?"

I stood marveling at her fearless expression of interest. I was on sensory overload. I doubted that I could have done what she was doing.

We watched a fine ophthalmologist who volunteers his time once a week to help anyone with eye problems, treating eyes for infection or other ailments.

And then there was Dr. Barbissi, a successful Christian

pharmacist who wanted to be a witness for Christ among his Muslim friends. Dr. Barbissi had been volunteering at the leper colony for twelve years. He told us that one day he was praying to know what more he could do for these men besides treating their sores. The impression came to him clearly that he should bathe them.

> *Charity is the pure love of Christ, and it endureth forever; and whoso is found possessed of it at the last day, it shall be well with him.*
>
> *Wherefore, . . . pray unto the Father with all the energy of heart, that ye may be filled with this love, which he hath bestowed upon all who are true followers of his Son, Jesus Christ.*
>
> MORONI 7:47–48

At first he was repulsed by the thought; but the thought would not leave him. So he began bathing them once a week. In the process he also gave them a shave and a haircut. After treating their sores with medication, he used foot powder and cream to prevent scabies. After bathing them, he would pray with them and give them a candy bar before sending them on their way.

We witnessed the literal realization of the doctrinal ideal of the pure love of Christ being put into practice. The impact was gigantic for me. We can speak of charity all day long. We can give sermons that encourage it. But until we manifest the pure love of Christ in our actions, our words are hollow:

"Charity is the pure love of Christ, and it endureth forever; and whoso is found possessed of it at the last day, it shall be well with him.

"Wherefore, . . . pray unto the Father with all the energy of heart, that ye may be filled with this love, which he hath bestowed upon all who are true followers of his Son, Jesus Christ" (Moroni 7:47–48).

I learned in that dusty desert about compassion. I learned that when we extend our hearts and hands toward others in Christlike love, something wonderful happens to us. I learned that when we serve others out of genuine love for the Lord and for our fellowmen, we are approaching the pure love of Christ.

You do not need to visit a leper colony to learn about charity. Each of us has stories that illustrate principles of compassion. Whether those stories come from antique family journals or from an afternoon's events, we need to take time to remember them and then share them or write them down.

Think about such an experience, why it was significant, and the reason it comes to mind. Remember, stories are powerful. Think about a memorable talk you have heard in general conference. It is likely it contains a story that illustrates a principle. It is stories that remain with us, bringing to mind again and again the point the speaker made. Share the stories in your life with those you love.

Chapter Eighteen

TRUE CONVERTING POWER

W. Craig Zwick

It is difficult to fully fathom the power of the Book of Mormon. But the following experiences have helped me understand a little more clearly that conversion to the Book of Mormon is conversion to the gospel of Jesus Christ.

The Book of Mormon has played a divine role in my life. I love the Book of Mormon. Let me tell you why. My father grew up in Salt Lake City but was not a member of the Church. His father, my grandfather, was a good man but wanted nothing to do with the Church or the missionaries. As a result, while he was growing up, my father was not allowed to participate in any Church activities or discussions.

When my father was seventeen years old, he met two missionaries in his neighborhood. Dad was inquisitive and bright, and he engaged the elders in conversation. He had some questions. He had been around many Latter-day Saints and had observed some things he couldn't quite understand.

These missionaries were wise. They answered his questions in a simple and succinct way, but then they testified of the truthfulness of the gospel of Jesus Christ. Their testimony touched my father's heart and planted a seed. He wanted to know more.

When Dad told his father that he would like to spend some time with the missionaries, his father told him in no uncertain terms that the missionaries were not welcome in the Zwick home. Because he respected his father so much, Dad reluctantly let the missionaries know he could not continue with the lessons.

Now these valiant missionaries were astute. They were not about to let a little thing like being banned from the home hinder their efforts.

It was December and Christmas was approaching, so they took a copy of the Book of Mormon and wrapped it with beautiful paper and ribbon. Inside they placed a card addressed to my father with a simple message that read, "Please read this book. It will change your life."

Knowing that their gift might be rejected if they delivered it, the elders asked someone else to drop it off for my father. Christmas was meager at the Zwick home, and so the gift was welcomed and put under the tree.

On Christmas morning my father opened the gift and took it to his room to begin reading. He read every day. He read with great interest and focus. The words penetrated his mind and heart, and he recognized that "the word of God is quick, and powerful, and sharper than any two-edged sword, piercing even to the dividing asunder of soul and spirit, and of the joints and marrow, and is a discerner of the thoughts and intents of the heart" (Hebrews 4:12). As he followed Moroni's admonition, the Spirit bore witness that the words were true, and my father knew what he must do. He sought the missionaries and asked them to teach him the lessons at the chapel. Because he loved and respected his father, Dad told him what he was doing and asked for his blessing. His father gave his reluctant permission but assured Dad that he would not be at his baptism. Just as my father was about to enter the baptismal font a short time later, however, his father walked in.

My father was converted to the Church because of the Book of Mormon. He knew of its truths before he had heard any of the supporting gospel lessons. I am profoundly grateful for my father's courage and faith. I cannot comprehend my life without the gospel of Jesus Christ. The Book of Mormon changed my father's life and as a result would change mine as well. Yes, I love the Book of Mormon.

The second story begins in Bolivia and ends in Bolivia but with a fair amount of time in between. Early one morning in the fall of 1968, my companion and I walked into the small adobe hospital in Tupiza, Bolivia. We were serving in the little villages of

Quiriza and Chacopampa but went to Tupiza every two weeks for food and mail. On this particular day, however, I needed something different. I needed a little emergency surgery.

Because there were no phones and we lived at least four days away from mission headquarters by ground, we couldn't get word

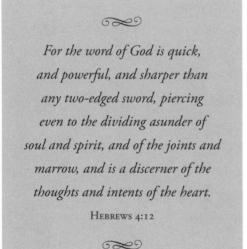

For the word of God is quick, and powerful, and sharper than any two-edged sword, piercing even to the dividing asunder of soul and spirit, and of the joints and marrow, and is a discerner of the thoughts and intents of the heart.

HEBREWS 4:12

to our mission president. We knew he would be concerned, but we didn't have a choice. It wasn't major surgery, but it would require me to stay in the hospital for a couple of days.

My companion, Elder Robert Dyer, and I took twenty copies of the Book of Mormon into the hospital to distribute. To make the copies more personal and to fill up my time while recuperating in the hospital bed, I pasted a photo of my family in each book and wrote beside the photo a brief testimony of my faith in Jesus Christ and of the truthfulness of the book.

At the end of my two-day stay in the hospital, all twenty copies of the Book of Mormon were gone. We hoped that they had made their way into the hands of those who would benefit from them.

Fast forward about eighteen years. I was now happily married with four wonderful children. Elder M. Russell Ballard, who had been my priests quorum adviser and bishop when I was a youth, asked me if I would like to accompany him to La Paz, Bolivia, where the first regional conference in Bolivia was to be held. Elder Ballard knew of my love for the Bolivian people and was aware that I was one of the first missionaries to serve in southern Bolivia.

What a sacred opportunity for me—to be back among the faithful Saints of Bolivia and to have the unique privilege of spending time with Elder Ballard. I knew I would be taught and tutored.

On a beautiful Saturday afternoon we walked into the La Paz Coliseum, filled to capacity for a priesthood leadership session. Many had come from outlying areas and had forded rivers and walked for days to attend. You could see the euphoria in their faces as they shook the hand of an Apostle of the Lord Jesus Christ.

Saints from seven stakes were involved in the conference, and Elder Ballard taught them well. During the leadership session he asked me to share my testimony. What an experience to look at so many faithful Saints, recognizing that only eighteen years prior, the Church was just beginning to emerge with branches, wards, and stakes only in embryo.

After the session, many priesthood leaders came forward to catch a glimpse of Elder Ballard. While I was waiting for him, a stake president from one of the seven stakes attending the conference introduced himself to me. He said he had something he wanted to show me. He took a copy of the Book of Mormon out of the canvas briefcase he was carrying. It was a well-worn copy— one of those blue paperback editions with an illustration of the angel Moroni on the cover.

He looked penetratingly into my eyes, handed it to me, and asked that I open it. I looked at him and then opened it to the title page. There I saw a water-damaged photo of my family and on the next page my handwritten testimony.

I was overcome with emotion and asked him to tell me his story. President Jose Adrian Velasco Chavez said:

"About fifteen years ago I was in the Tupiza Hospital waiting to see a doctor. On the table was a blue book. I picked it up and glanced through it. The person at the desk told me I could take it. It was free. I took it to my home in Tupiza and placed it on a bookshelf, without reading it.

"Years later I was offered employment in La Paz and moved there with my family. While unpacking, I noticed the book again. I set it aside with every intention of just throwing it away but never did.

"One evening I saw the book and picked it up. I opened it and read your testimony. That intrigued me, so I began reading the first page and soon realized that this was no ordinary book.

"This sacred volume of scripture touched my heart. It was

about my people. It had answers to my questions. I prayed fervently to know if it was true. As I came to know of the divinity of the book, I introduced my wife and children to it.

"The missionaries taught us, but we already had firm testimonies of the gospel of Jesus Christ because of this sacred and powerful book. I don't know how it got into that hospital, but I thank my Heavenly Father every day that I found this precious book."

Though I was thrilled to hear his story, it isn't about me. It is about the Book of Mormon and its converting power.

For each of us to comprehend the value of this book,

> *The convincing and converting powers of the Book of Mormon come from both a central focus upon the Lord Jesus Christ and the inspired plainness and clarity of its teachings.*
>
> Elder David A. Bednar[1]

we must read it, learn its truths, and incorporate them into our lives. My love for the Book of Mormon is ever increasing.

May these stories inspire you to write and share your own conversion stories. May the powerful witness of the Savior contained in the Book of Mormon be a constant source of spiritual energy for you and your posterity as it has been for ours.

Chapter Nineteen

His Hands

W. Craig Zwick

Thirty-two years ago our tiny newborn son Spencer struggled for his life in the neonatal intensive care unit of Primary Children's Medical Center in Salt Lake City. Because of his premature birth, his lungs were not fully developed, and he desperately fought for each breath of air. Nine years earlier we had been in the same intensive care unit, where our eldest son, Scott, also premature, struggled for his life.

Indelibly imprinted in my mind are the rows of small, transparent incubators used for premature babies. I remember how tiny the babies were, some not even two pounds. There were medical machines and tubes and nurses totally devoted and focused on these infants. I will never forget the worried looks on the faces of the mothers and fathers who stood vigilant with a prayer in their hearts at each of the incubators.

Spencer was one of these babies, and we were as concerned as the other parents. He was so small but had so much will to live. Each breath was like blowing up a balloon and then letting the air out. When the air went out of his little lungs, his entire abdomen collapsed. Each breath took every bit of energy and determination to live that our struggling little boy had.

We prayed that the Lord's hand would reach out and somehow help our son continue to breathe. As I put my trembling hands through the small opening of the incubator, I felt so inadequate and powerless. I took hold of the tiny but perfect hand of our newborn son and felt a powerful spiritual connection never to be forgotten. Two fingers from each of my hands covered his tiny head as I administered to him.

Our desire for him was pure, but we knew that his earthly experience rested in the Lord's hands and not in ours or in the medical team that cared for him. I then humbly realized that my quivering hands held power and authority well beyond my own. My fingers on his head symbolized the placing of God's hands and power upon our son.

Following the blessing, in a moment of emotional peace, my eternal companion and I looked at each other across the incubator, feeling the spirit of renewed hope and comfort born of faith in the Lord Jesus Christ and in the personal effect of His Atonement.

It was a powerful witness of His love for an infant son who

had just left His presence. We were then better prepared to accept His will for our son. We truly felt we had placed our hands in the hands of the Savior. It was as if the Savior's own hands provided the critical respiratory aid, allowing our son to breathe and gain enough strength to survive.

Three weeks later we took Spencer home from the hospital. He weighed almost five pounds. It was a miracle to us. But that very evening as my wife was holding him, she felt an unusual lump on his back. Our worst fears were realized, and our precious baby went back to the hospital to have a tumor removed from his spine.

We knew we could go forward in the strength of the Lord. We put our hands in His, and we felt His sustaining presence. Once again I knew that I had been entrusted with the greatest power on earth, and as I put my hands on Spencer's tiny head to give him yet another blessing, I felt the Lord's help.

The Lord knows us, but He may choose to answer our prayers in different ways. Other tumors appeared in different locations. Two more surgeries followed, and although heavy concerns crowded our hearts, we once again felt the hand of the Lord. Little Spencer had been given priesthood blessings, and his name had been written on prayer rolls and voiced in pleadings by family and friends. These are the strengths we drew upon. We never felt alone. The spirit and power of God rested upon us, and faith filled our souls.

Today we, along with our healthy son, continue to be deeply grateful for the Savior's merciful hands.

The great plan of happiness includes a proverbial roller coaster of challenging times along with the joyful times. Yes, we all have our moments of difficulty and heartbreak. Occasionally they are so difficult for us that we just want to give up. There are times when our steps are unsteady, when we feel discouraged, and when we cry out in desperation.

From these experiences with an infant son struggling for his life, I learned that I

> *Adored is the hand that saves—even the hand of Jesus Christ, the Son of God. . . . With that hand he knocks upon the door of our understanding.*
> PRESIDENT THOMAS S. MONSON[1]

must extend my hand and connect to the comfort provided by a loving Heavenly Father and His Son, Jesus Christ. They will provide sustenance and support if we are willing to open the door and receive their hands of divine assistance.

During those many lonely nights spent in the neonatal intensive care unit of Primary Children's Medical Center, I learned that our loving Heavenly Father provides sustaining and comforting companionship. I learned that His will is most clearly manifest when we have done all we can do and then faithfully place our hands in His and our confidence and trust in Him.

I learned the richness of meaningful fasting and prayer and the power of the priesthood. I learned to accept very slow progress and to be grateful for each incremental bit of positive change. Sometimes that progress is so small that it's hard to imagine it as positive at all.

Because Spencer is our youngest child, his three older brothers and sister learned to better understand the power of the priesthood and the effectiveness of fasting and prayer. They also learned to place their own hands in the hands of the Savior. Yes, they shared a powerful bond with their little brother, and they also shared a powerful bond with their Heavenly Father and His son.

Imagine the wounds in the Savior's weathered hands. His hands of torn flesh and physical sacrifice give our own hands greater power, more meaningful use, and clearer direction.

It is the wounded Christ who leads us through our moments of difficulty. It is He who bears us up when we need more air to breathe or more direction to follow or even more courage to continue.

I testify that if we will keep the commandments of God and walk hand in hand with Him in His paths, we will go forward with faith and never feel alone.

THEREFORE, WHAT?

W. Craig Zwick and Jan J. Zwick

Grandpa Johnson had quite an imagination. While our children were growing up, they spent countless hours listening to his imaginative stories and his real-life adventures. Sitting in his brown leather chair or finding a comfortable place outside, he would gather his grandchildren around him and pour out the most amazing tales.

At the conclusion of each one, he never failed to ask, "So what did you learn from this story?" or "What is the moral of this experience?" He would then patiently listen to his grandchildren talk about the significant things they had discovered while listening to his remarkable accounts.

He told stories about his youth, about growing up in the Depression, about his mission, and about his parents and grandparents. He also regaled his grandchildren with magical stories of adventure and mystery. They never wanted the stories to end.

And guess what? Even decades later our children still remember the stories—memories that give them understanding and strength. The stories were not only interesting but also instructive. Our children were taught ideals of hard work, faith, and hope, and of using talents, overcoming adversity, and showing compassion. Those stories connected them to their ancestors and taught them rich lessons about family values and beliefs.

> *Treasure up in your minds continually the words of life.*
>
> DOCTRINE & COVENANTS 84:85

We need stories! We need stories to give meaning to facts. We need stories to help us remember important events and to expand our thoughts and sympathy. Stories cause us to think and to feel. Stories reinforce important values in our lives. When we tell others of our experiences, we are inviting them onto the sacred ground of our memories and hearts.

Our experiences make us who we are, but until we tell about ourselves and share our stories, others may know little about us. What might a teenage son learn as he listens to his father tell of his mission experiences? What might a new mother learn from her own mother's feelings of being a mother for the first time? We should take pleasure in sharing something of ourselves so that those we love will know more about us.

Relating personal experiences can have a powerful influence on those around us, especially on our family members and those we teach in our Church responsibilities. Sharing experiences creates an unmeasured reward of satisfaction and understanding that serves the listener as well as the teller. This strengthens the connection between them.

THEREFORE, WHAT?

We know that stories are powerful tools, but where do we go from here? What do we do with our stories? How do we apply principles to real-life experiences?

In this book we have shared some of our experiences and what we have learned from them. Now it is your turn to do something with your stories. The process is simple, which makes it achievable for each of us. To get started, consider the following suggestions.

PONDER

Think about five experiences or stories that have stuck in your mind over the years. They could have to do with your childhood, parents, ancestors, or children. Perhaps one of those experiences is an event that has taken place in the kitchen, at the dining table, or on a vacation. Maybe it is funny. Maybe it is sad. It might be about an object or a family hero or a family tradition. The events that shape your character and make you who you are can be tools in the hands of the Lord. Everyone has great material for storytelling. As you begin this process, your first thoughts will likely imbue you with tremendous energy. Once you have started, you will be eager to continue.

IDENTIFY PRINCIPLES

There is a reason these five experiences have had such an effect on you. What was the object or driving force? What did the experiences teach you? How did you feel? Did they motivate you to be better or to do something differently? Did they touch your heart, or did you feel the Spirit?

What principles come to mind when you think of these experiences? As you identify the principles taught by personal experiences, the Spirit will expand your understanding. Pay close attention to spiritual confirmations. Remember the Lord's statement: "All things unto me are spiritual" (D&C 29:34). If we prayerfully seek them, we can find spiritual lessons in even the simplest events.

SHARE

Share your stories by writing them down or recounting them to others. It might be helpful to jot down a few of the simple details of the story and the feelings associated with your experience. Convey your thoughts on the principles you learned.

You don't want just a collection of random facts, but you do want to capture the essence of what really happened. Surrounding the dinner table during the evening meal or during a family home evening would be a good place to share.

These stories can become an important part of your family history. When we open

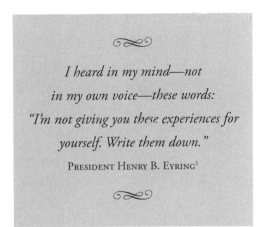

I heard in my mind—not in my own voice—these words: "I'm not giving you these experiences for yourself. Write them down."

PRESIDENT HENRY B. EYRING[1]

our hearts and share our stories with others, we can strengthen faith and courage in others and in ourselves. We can also reinforce gospel principles as we "treasure up in [our] minds continually the words of life" (D&C 84:85).

True stories of faith and achievement are part of the spiritual and cultural heritage we pass on to our children. As Alma reminds Helaman, written records "have enlarged the memory of this people" (Alma 37:8).

President Henry B. Eyring shared an experience that taught him the importance of recording personal memories. He recounted: "When our children were very small, I started to write down a few things about what happened every day. Let me tell you how that got started. I came home late from a Church assignment. It was after dark. My father-in-law, who lived near us, surprised me as I walked toward the front door of my house. He was carrying a load of pipes over his shoulder, walking very fast and dressed in his work clothes. I knew that he had been building a system to pump water from a stream below us up to our property.

"He smiled, spoke softly, and then rushed past me into the darkness to go on with his work. I took a few steps toward the house, thinking of what he was doing for us, and just as I got to the door, I heard in my mind—not in my own voice—these words: 'I'm not giving you these experiences for yourself. Write them down.'

"I went inside. I didn't go to bed. Although I was tired, I took out some paper and began to write. And as I did, I understood the message I had heard in my mind. I was supposed to record for my children to read, someday in the future, how I had seen the hand of God blessing our family. Grandpa didn't have to do what he was doing for us. He could have had someone else do it or not have done it at all. But he was serving us, his family, in the way covenant disciples of Jesus Christ always do. I knew that was true. And so I wrote it down, so that my children could have the memory someday when they would need it."

Writing down experiences helps us remember them longer and allows us to share them with greater accuracy. By keeping memories alive with stories, we connect the challenges and solutions of earlier generations to some of the trials we currently face. President Gordon B. Hinckley reminded us:

"It is good to look to the past to gain appreciation for the present and perspective for the future. It is good to look upon the virtues of those who have gone before, to gain strength for whatever lies ahead. It is good to reflect upon the work of those who labored so hard and gained so little in this world, but out of whose dreams and early plans, so well nurtured, has come a great harvest of which we are the beneficiaries. Their tremendous example can become a compelling motivation for us all, for each of us is a pioneer in his own life."

> *It is good to look to the past to gain appreciation for the present and perspective for the future. It is good to look upon the virtues of those who have gone before, to gain strength for whatever lies ahead. . . . Their tremendous example can become a compelling motivation for us all, for each of us is a pioneer in his own life.*
>
> PRESIDENT GORDON B. HINCKLEY[2]

We hope that you can see why stories are valuable. We have not mentioned all the ways personal experiences convey values and open doors of understanding, but we hope we have planted a seed—a seed that will begin to grow and expand your vision of the importance of recording and sharing your experiences and feelings through stories. For we promise you, there is more to our story and more to yours.

We also promise that your storytelling experiences will be satisfying and inspirational. They will have a lasting effect for generations and will positively change lives, including your own. In the end, one of the most effective ways we teach each other is through principle-based stories that include our personal treasures from real-life experiences.

Notes

Chapter One: The Awakening

1. Postman, "Learning by Story," *Atlantic Monthly,* December 1989, 122.

Chapter Three: A Time of Reflection

1. "They, the Builders of the Nation," *Hymns of The Church of Jesus Christ of Latter-day Saints* (Salt Lake City: The Church of Jesus Christ of Latter-day Saints, 1985), no. 36.

Chapter Six: Everything to Do with the Spirit

1. Ballard, "Now Is the Time," *Ensign,* November 2000, 75.
2. Pearce, *A Heart like His* (Salt Lake City: Deseret Book, 2006), 81.

Chapter Nine: Negative Painting

1. Swenson, available at http://brendaswenson.blogspot.com/2012/03 negative-painting-with-watercolor.html.

NOTES

2. Whitney, in Spencer W. Kimball, *Faith Precedes the Miracle* (Salt Lake City: Deseret Book, 1972), 98.

3. Swenson.

CHAPTER TEN: BECOMING

1. Uchtdorf, "Christlike Attributes—the Wind beneath Our Wings," *Ensign,* November 2005, 102; paragraphing altered.

CHAPTER ELEVEN: SWEET BOLDNESS

1. *Preach My Gospel: A Guide to Missionary Service* (Salt Lake City: The Church of Jesus Christ of Latter-day Saints, 2004), 115.

2. Smith, *Gospel Doctrine* (Salt Lake City: Deseret Book, 1939), 251–52.

CHAPTER TWELVE: EXAMPLE, EXAMPLE, EXAMPLE

1. "True to the Faith," *Hymns of The Church of Jesus Christ of Latter-day Saints* (Salt Lake City: The Church of Jesus Christ of Latter-day Saints, 1985), no. 254.

CHAPTER THIRTEEN: TEACH BY EXAMPLE

1. Young, *Discourses of Brigham Young,* comp. John A. Widtsoe (Salt Lake City: Deseret Book, 1954), 208.

2. Benson, "Worthy Sons, Worthy Fathers," *Ensign,* November 1985, 35.

CHAPTER FOURTEEN: CHOICES

1. Scott, "Using the Supernal Gift of Prayer," *Ensign,* May 2007, 9.

2. Scott, "Using the Supernal Gift of Prayer," *Ensign,* May 2007, 11.

CHAPTER FIFTEEN: I KNOW I CAN

1. Ballard, "Do Things That Make a Difference," *Ensign,* June 1983, 69.

CHAPTER EIGHTEEN: TRUE CONVERTING POWER

1. Bednar, "Watching with All Perseverance," *Ensign,* May 2010, 40.

NOTES

Chapter Nineteen: His Hands

1. Monson, "Hands," *Ensign,* August 1990, 5.

Conclusion: "Therefore, What?"

1. Eyring, "O Remember, Remember," *Ensign,* November 2007, 66–67.
2. Hinckley, "The Faith of the Pioneers," *Ensign,* July 1984, 3.

INDEX

INDEX

INDEX

ABOUT THE AUTHORS

ELDER W. CRAIG ZWICK was sustained as a member of the First Quorum of the Seventy of The Church of Jesus Christ of Latter-day Saints on April 1, 1995. He served as president of the North America Northeast Area, the Brazil Area, and the Brazil South Area and in the presidencies of the Europe West Area and Europe Central Area. Previous to his calling as a General Authority, he served as president of the Chile Santiago South Mission. He was also a full-time missionary in the Argentina North Mission.

Before his full-time Church service, Elder Zwick was president and CEO of Zwick Construction Company, which built the Portland Oregon Temple and, in Salt Lake City, the Church History Museum, the Family History Library, and the South Visitors' Center on Temple Square. The company also built schools, hospitals, and shopping centers in California and

Utah. Elder Zwick served as a member of the board of directors of the Associated General Contractors of America and was director of the Utah State Department of Transportation. He received a degree in business management and finance from the University of Utah, where he met his wife, Jan. They are the parents of four children and grandparents of fifteen. Elder and Sister Zwick both speak fluent Spanish and Portuguese.

SISTER JAN J. ZWICK has served in a variety of callings in the Church, including ward and stake Young Women president and member of the Young Women general board. She was a full-time missionary with her husband and children in the Chile Santiago South Mission. She served as a member of the Disabilities Committee of the Church and of the Utah Easter Seals board. In recent years she has developed a talent and love for watercolor painting.